BEFORE CHERNOBYL

Nuclear Accidents the World has Forgotten

By Nick Brazil

Revised First edition published in the United Kingdom in 2021 by Brazil Productions, The Mount, Hardwick Road, Whitchurch-on-Thames, Reading RG8 7HW.

ISBN 978-1-9163998-0-8

First edition published in 2021
This book has been lodged with The Agency for The Legal Deposit Libraries.

Cover Phototgraph by Doroshvin/Shutterstock

Acknowledgements

I owe a number of people a great debt of gratitude for helping me complete this book in different ways. Firstly there is Jerry Cockram and Katherine Higley who took on the onerous task of proof reading the manuscript with a forensic and creative approach that greatly improved the final book. I am very grateful to Tamara Schiopu for providing the chapter on her first hand experiences living next door to a nuclear disaster. Joseph Thomas' help was invaluable in providing his photographs and first hand account of the B.52 crash at Thule in Greenland. I am also very grateful to Gianluca Pisanello of First Light Fusion Ltd not only for providing the image of an artist's impression of a fusion energy plant but also for his help and advice on fusion energy. Many thanks to D.P. for her advice on nuclear power. I would also like to pay tribute to three authors of works that provided invaluable research information for this book. Firstly, the late Ralph E. Lapp, author of *The Voyage of The Lucky Dragon*, the detailed and highly readable story of the Japanese tuna fisherman irradiated by the Castle Bravo bomb. Secondly, Dirk Septer whose book *Lost Nuke - The Last Flight of Bomber 075* provided a fascinating insight into America's first Broken Arrow incident. Thirdly, Kristen Iversen, whose book *Full Body Burden: Growing Up in the Nuclear Shadow of Rocky Flats* gave a very comprehensive account of the complex history of the Rocky Flats Nuclear Plant. Last, but certainly not least, I am indebted to my son Peter for his support and encouragement during the time I spent writing this book.

This book is dedicated to all victims of Nuclear Accidents,
especially those who risked their lives
fighting to control them.

About the Author

Nick Brazil, who was born in Looe, Cornwall, is an author, film maker, photographer and public speaker. He has worked and travelled in Southern Africa, the Middle East and North and South America. His photographs have been published by the Oxford University Press and Time/Life. He has made eight documentaries including the award winning Mr Toad's Village. *Before Chernobyl* is the fourth book he has published. He lives in Oxfordshire, U.K.

Other Books by Nick Brazil:

A Journey With Ghosts

Cheating Death
a.k.a. Suicide on Whit Sunday

Billy Biscuit - The Colourful Life & Times
of Sir William Curtis

Contents

A Child of the Nuclear Age

As someone who was born and brought up in the mid 1950s, I have always had a fascination with Nuclear Power and energy. Vivid childhood memories of the Cold War and fear of nuclear attack still inform my thinking about this period. Indeed, I clearly remember many of the catastrophic events described in the following pages. Which brings me to the purpose of this book.

As well as being a potted history of the major nuclear disasters that have occurred over the past seventy-eight years it shows how and why they happened. It also examines the long term consequences of such events. More importantly perhaps, it asks if lessons have been learned and if such catastrophes can ever happen again.

I have deliberately excluded the two most recent major nuclear catastrophes at Chernobyl and Fukushima since they have been extensively covered elsewhere. My concern is to look in detail at all the other nuclear accidents that have occurred since 1942. These also include nuclear accidents involving aircraft and naval vessels.

It is important to note that this book is not intended as an attack on the nuclear industry any more than a book about airline safety is an attack on flying. It's primary purpose is to be a history of these largely forgotten or unknown nuclear incidents.

Nick Brazil

Whitchurch-on-Thames, February 2021

Some Explanations

Nuclear energy is a complex subject, so the following explanations are designed to help the reader to understand the various incidents described in this book.

Atom

An atom is the smallest unit of ordinary matter. Everything, whether it is solid, liquid, gas or plasma is composed of atoms.

Chain Reaction

When the neutrons of an atom hit another they are absorbed into its mass and create more neutrons.The newly created neutrons then fly off and repeat the process multiple times. A chain reaction is this process involving many thousands if not millions of atoms and neutrons invisible to the naked eye and occurring in a split second. This process creates energy and heat. A nuclear chain reaction is triggered when two quantities of fissile material such as uranium-235 combine to reach a critical mass (see below).

Criticality Accident

An uncontrolled chain reaction caused by the accidental accumulation of fissile materials such as uranium or plutonium in a critical mass. See Chapter 6 - *A Question of Criticality*.

Critical Mass

The smallest amount of fissile material such as uranium needed to create a chain reaction.

Control Rods

These are the "accelerator and brake" mechanism that control the speed of a chain reaction in a nuclear reactor. As their name suggests they are rods made of materials such as boron, cadmium, silver, and/or indium which have an ability to absorb the neutrons produced in a chain reaction. The rods are inserted into the nuclear reactor where the chain reaction is taking place. The further they go the more neutrons are absorbed slowing down the chain reaction process. If they are removed, the process is reversed and the chain reaction speeds up.

Heavy Water

This type of water only contains deuterium also known as heavy hydrogen rather than the hydrogen - 1 isotope also known as protium which comprises the bulk of normal water. This makes heavy water much heavier than normal water. Although it occurs naturally, heavy water is very rare in this state. So, to produce it in any significant quantity repeated electrolysis of normal water is used. This requires hundreds of gallons or litres of water from which small quantities of heavy water are produced. Heavy water is used in the nuclear industry as an ideal medium for slowing neutrons down and can be used to control nuclear chain reactions. Neutrons are an integral part of the chain reaction process.

International Nuclear Event Scale (INES)

This is the measurement of severity of a nuclear event/accident. It was devised in 1990 by the International Nuclear Energy Agency to give a measurement of the magnitude of nuclear events. The INES scale has seven levels with 1 being the lowest (i.e. cracks and leaks in a reactor housing) and 7 the highest (i.e. Chernobyl - major disaster with multiple fatalities and injuries).

Nuclear Power

This is the use of nuclear reactions created by combining materials such as uranium in certain quantities that spark and start a chain reaction as described previously. The quantities of uranium required for this to happen are known as a critical mass. The chain reaction releases nuclear energy which generates a huge amount of heat. This is most commonly used in nuclear power stations to produce steam in turbines which then power turbines to produce electricity.

Nuclear Core or Capsule

Consisting of a plutonium globe, this is the "heart" of a nuclear weapon and is used to trip the series of triggers that lead to a nuclear explosion.

Neutrons

These are sub atomic (i.e. minuscule) particles produced by a chain reaction. As such they are the drivers of the process. The more they are removed from the process using control rods the slower the process becomes.

Plutonium

This radioactive metal that only appears in nature as a trace element. It is generally manufactured from uranium 238 in nuclear plants for use as a fuel in nuclear energy and part of the explosive process in nuclear weapons. It is pyrophoric, which means it can ignite when in contact with air, water or hydrogen.

Chapter 1
The First Nuclear Accident
Leipzig L-IV Experimental Reactor
Leipzig, Germany
June 23, 1942

Most people would be very surprised to learn that the world's first nuclear accident did not occur in Great Britain or America but in the heart of Hitler's Germany. In the summer of 1942, a team of German nuclear scientists led by Werner Heisenberg had developed an experimental nuclear reactor called L-IV in their Leipzig laboratory. As early as 1938, this team under Heisenberg had been working towards creating a nuclear bomb. L-IV was the latest stage of this project.

Born in the Bavarian city of Würzburg in 1901, Heisenberg was probably Germany's most brilliant physicist. He showed early promise in this field when, aged only 24, he published a groundbreaking paper on quantum mechanics. This was the first of many achievements in a life that would be devoted to physics. Not the least of his early achievements was to be awarded The Nobel Peace Prize in 1932 for his work on quantum mechanics.

However, he did not spend all his time cloistered away in laboratories. During the turbulent period following Germany's defeat in World War One, he joined the *Freikorps*. Made up of a mixture of former soldiers, mercenaries and political idealists, this was a paramilitary group closely aligned with the Weimar Republic. Heisenberg's motivation for joining was to bring down The Bavarian Soviet Republic in 1918 -19.

In 1922, he met the Danish nuclear physicist Niels Bohr which proved to be a watershed event that would shape the rest of his life. By the mid to late 1930s, Heisenberg was pre-eminent in the field of nuclear physics. He may not have known it then, but Hitler's new Nazi regime would soon play an important part in his life.

Curiously, many leading members of the Nazi Party did not cherish Germany's brilliant scientists like Heisenberg. In fact, they seemed to regard them as secret enemies of the Reich. This led to a personal attack on Heisenberg in the SS newspaper *Black Corps* which called him a White Jew who should 'disappear'.

However, he survived this and a subsequent SS investigation, probably because enough influential Nazis appreciated his value to the Reich. At the outbreak of the Second World War, Heisenberg was a member of the *Uranverein,* the German nuclear weapons programme. It was during this time and before, that Werner Heisenberg and his colleagues including Robert Dopel developed the experimental nuclear reactor called L-IV.

On 23rd June 1942, a leak of heavy water was discovered in the protective jacket of this Leipzig reactor. During the inspection, air leaked into the nuclear pile setting the uranium powder inside alight. This immediately caused a violent conflagration boiling the cooling water in the reactor and blowing it apart. Particles of the uranium heated to a temperature of 1000 degrees centigrade shot up six metres to the ceiling and showered across the laboratory building.

After this explosion, which destroyed the reactor, Heisenberg and his team would continue to work on nuclear reactions right up to the end of the war. He was also involved in the country's weapons programme in other ways as well.

In June 1942, he was called to a meeting with Albert Speer, Hitler's Minister for Armaments to discuss the development of the German A-bomb. Heisenberg had the unenviable task of telling Speer that limitations of manpower and materials meant a nuclear bomb could not be built before 1945. Was Heisenberg simply being practical and 'telling truth to power'? Or perhaps this was a desperate ploy to prevent the Nazis from getting nuclear weapons for as long as possible.

Heisenberg certainly believed nuclear weapons could be developed. Whether he *actually* wanted an A-bomb in Nazi hands or he simply wanted to develop nuclear fission for energy is an open question. Strangely but fortuitously, much of the Nazi heirarchy did not appear to understand the potency of such a weapon. In 1943 the *Uranverein* was diverted from work on nuclear weapons to nuclear power which was considered more important to the war effort.

This must have delayed the development of Hitler's A-bomb for a crucial period. Had this not happened, Nazi Germany rather than the Americans could well have dropped the first A-bomb in anger. The effect on the course of The Second World War would have been incalculable.

At the end of the war, Heisenberg was captured by the Allies. He spent a lengthy period of interrogation by British Intelligence in Farm Hall an intelligence 'safe house' in Godmanchester, Cambridgeshire. To find out what he and the other German scientists really knew, British Intelligence had bugged the building.

Unsurprisingly, the recordings revealed that all the scientists were pleased the Allies had won the War. What Heisenberg said was more revealing:

"We wouldn't have had the moral courage to recommend to the Government in the spring of 1942 that they should employ 120,000 men just for building the thing up."

Heisenberg was finally allowed back to Germany where he was reunited with his family. He resumed his career in scientific research and development which he pursued for the rest of his life. This included the establishment of Germany's first nuclear reactor in 1957. He died in Munich of kidney failure at the age of 74. The Leipzig L-IV explosion was the first nuclear accident in history.

Werner Heisenberg in 1933
Photograph: Bundesarchiv, Bild 183-R57262

Members of Project Alsos dismantling the German Experimental Pile - Haigerloch, Germany - April 1945.
Photograph Mickey Thurgood, U. S. Army photographer assigned to Alsos Mission

Tailpiece
The Alsos Mission

In September 1943, the Allied Forces invaded Italy to begin their long slog to retake that difficult and mountainous country from the Germans. At this time U.S. Brigadier General Wilhelm B, Styer who was Chief of Staff of Army Service Forces, became worried that vital information about enemy nuclear weapons programmes was not being gathered systematically. The danger was that ‘greenhorns’ stumbling on vital bits of information would simply discard them out of ignorance. He figured that a dedicated and knowledgeable team was needed to search out this material so that it was not simply scattered and lost.

With the backing of General George Marshall, Chief of Staff of the U.S. Army, he took this idea to Brigadier General Leslie Groves who was in charge of the *Manhattan Project* to develop the American atom bomb. Groves’ response was to create the Alsos Mission dedicated to tracking down as much information, material and personnel as possible related to the Nazi nuclear and biological weapons programme. The man put in charge of the Mission was Lieutenant Colonel Boris Pash who had a background in counter intelligence. One of his jobs had been to investigate a Soviet spy ring at the Radiation Laboratory at Berkeley, University of California.

Following closely on the heels of the invading Allied Forces, Alsos would scour freshly liberated parts of Europe for anything related to this ultra secret aspect of the Nazi war effort. This was considered to be a matter of urgency on two counts. Firstly, to prevent the Germans from developing and using an A-bomb or biological weapon against Great Britain and the allies. Secondly to stop their scientists and secret weapons falling into Soviet hands. Officially, Stalin’s Russia might still have been our ally against Nazi Germany at this time but it was already clear she would be the new enemy after Hitler’s defeat.

The first port of call for the Alsos Mission was Italy where they landed in December 1943. Frustratingly, in spite of interviewing leading members of the Italian Provisional Government and the country’s top scientists, they found little of value. Already a picture was emerging of a far less advanced German nuclear war programme than that envisaged by the allies.

In December 1943 Alsos set up a liaison office in London with two officers, two WAC clerks and three intelligence agents. Their job was to sift through intelligence documents and photographs to assess how far the German nuclear weapons project had processed. For example, they would examine aerial photographs of uranium and thorium mines in Sudetenland (now part of the Czech Republic) to see how fast the piles of mining waste had grown. This would tell them how much of those two minerals, vital in the production of nuclear weapons had been mined.

In France, the Alsos Team pursued top French physicists including Frédéric Joliot-Curie who had been working for the Germans, They eventually caught up with him at his laboratory in the College de France. Alsos also had priority intelligence targets in Belgium with large quantities of uranium from the mines in the Belgian Congo stored at a processing plant near Antwerp. Although they found 68 tons there, another 1000 tons had gone to Germany and a further 80 tons to occupied France. They finally tracked down 31 tons of that consignment, but the remaining 49 tons were never found.

As the Allied Forces fought across occupied Europe towards Germany, the Alsos team followed, first to Strasbourg capturing a German nuclear laboratory in the grounds of the local hospital and finally into Germany itself. Whilst they found many scientists and documents, they discovered no nuclear weapons.

Eventually, they captured most of the German scientists down in Bavaria along with their equipment. This included Heisenberg's experimental reactor at his laboratory in the medieval city of Haigerloch.

As well as this hardware, the Mission's haul included a centrifuge and 260 truckloads of uranium ore, sodium uranate and ferrouranium weighing about 1,000 tons. Often operating at breakneck speed and sometimes under fire, the Alsos Mission's accomplishments were not inconsiderable. Hoewever, not everyone was overwhelmed by what they discovered.

Samuel Goudsmit, the Chief Scientific Advisor attached to the Alsos Mission felt that the German nuclear effort had been incredibly small scale and Heath Robinsonian when compared to the *Manhattan Project*. In Goudsmit's eyes it amounted to little more than some laboratories occupying a small cave, part of a textile factory and some rooms in a disused brewery. He was probably right in his estimation that Alsos cost more than the whole German nuclear programme.

The fact that the Nazis failed to grasp the full importance of nuclear weapons ensured that the world had a very lucky escape.

Chapter 2
Kazakhstan's Nightmare Legacy
1949 - 1991

The Soviet Union exploded its first nuclear bomb in Kazakhstan in 1949. Codenamed *Operation First Lightning*, it was hailed as a glorious step forward in the fight against capitalism by Soviet dictator Joseph Stalin. In reality, it marked the start of a human tragedy that continues to this day.

The location for the Russian nuclear test site was chosen by Lavrentiy Beria in 1947. As well as being head of the KGB, he was the political boss of the Soviet atomic weapons project at the time. The area he marked out was 18,000 square kilometres (11,160 square miles) of steppes in the North Eastern part of the Kazakhstan Soviet Socialist Republic. At the time he described the area as uninhabited. In fact, it was the home of many thousands of people who would suffer immeasurably from the nuclear tests conducted in that area over the next forty years.

The infrastructure for the test complex was constructed using forced labour from *gulags*. It took its name Semipalatinsk-21 from the main city about 150 kilometres away. In total, the Russian military conducted 456 nuclear tests at the site of which 116 were atmospheric. At no time were any of the 200,000 inhabitants of the many villages and towns in the area evacuated.

Quite the opposite in fact. Today, eyewitnesses tell visiting journalists how the authorities ordered them to stand outside their homes when tests were conducted. Apparently, this was so scientists could examine them for damage done to their bodies by radiation from the explosions (1).

Today's legacy of this abominably cruel attitude to the local population can be seen in the many deformed children lying abandoned in Kazakhstan's orphanages. It is estimated that as many as one in twenty children in the area are born with horrible malformations. It is also estimated that 50% of the population of the Semey (Formerly Semipalatinsk) Oblast die before the age of sixty(1).

In a very upsetting report from Kazakhstan in 2007, CNN journalist Matthew Chance described how he saw small children with huge heads on tiny bodies and others with unnaturally twisted limbs lying in orphanage cots. All of them were the victims of radiation from Kazakhstan's tests (2). The last nuclear test was conducted at the Semipalatisk site in 1989 and it was officially closed in 1991. For some years after that it was left in a deserted state with large amounts of radioactive waste scattered around the area. The health and security implications of this were of considerable international concern.

From 1995 until 2012 a joint operation by Kazakh, Russian and American scientists cleared up much of this radioactive waste at a cost of $(US)150 million. Tragically, significant areas of the old test complex remain heavily irradiated. The missiles and nuclear bombs may have now vanished from this remote part of Central Asia, but the terrible legacy of birth defects will probably remain forever.

Footnote

Atomic Lake

One highly visible legacy of the test programme is Lake Chagan which was created by a 140 kiloton nuclear explosion in January 1965. Unlike the other tests at the Kazakh test site, this particular explosion had a peaceful purpose. It was part of the Soviet programme called Nuclear Explosions for The National Economy which involved using nuclear blasts for massive earth moving projects.

The lake now holds 350 million cubic feet of water which is supplied by a tributary of the River Irtysh. How much use this must be for drinking and irrigation purposes is surely questionable since Chagan is still radioactive earning it the nickname Atomic Lake.

Project Plowshare

The U.S. Government had a similar programme for the peaceful use of nuclear explosions called Project Plowshare. Between 1962 and 1977 thirty-one nuclear warheads were detonated in twenty-seven separate tests at the Yucca Flats in Nevada National Security Site. One of the biggest was the Sedan Test in 1962 which was responsible for radioactively contaminating more people than any other nuclear test. Like the Chagan test in Kazakhstan, it left a permanent scar on the landscape in the form of a huge crater whose explosive creation displaced 11,000,000 tons of earth. It is listed on The National Register of Historic Places and is open for visitors' tours. Dangerous side effects such as excessive radiation forced the cessation of Project Plowshare in 1977.

Map showing location of the Soviet Union's nuclear test site of Semipalatinsk in North Eastern Kazakhstan. *Created by Finlay McWalter*

'Stronger than Death' Memorial to the victims of Semipalatinsk Nuclear Test Site on Polkovnichi island in Semey {The new name for Semipalatinsk), Kazakhstan
Photograph: Nina Alizada/Shutterstock

Chapter 3
When the Sun Rose in the West
The Lucky Dragon Incident and Bikini Tests
22nd January - March 1954

A keen wind blew across the harbour on that cold January day in 1954. Tied to the quay was the tuna fishing boat *The Lucky Dragon Number 5.* On board her crew were busily preparing the vessel for the long trip to the Pacific fishing grounds. This would take them thousands of miles from their home port of Yaizu in the central Japanese prefecture of Shizuoka 120 miles to the south of Tokyo.

On the quayside a group of wives, family members and girlfriends of the 23 crew had gathered to see the boat off on her first fishing trip of the year. No doubt the well wishers had mixed feelings. *The Lucky Dragon* would be gone for nearly three months as she searched for the elusive but valuable shoals of blue finned tuna across that vast ocean. The families knew there was always a chance their loved ones would never return, their vessels having sunk beneath the mountainous waves of a terrifying Pacific storm.

On board *The Lucky Dragon* morale was high amongst the crew including their twenty-three year old captain Hisakichi Tsutsui. After all, this was the first trip of the year and the vessel's new name would surely bring good fortune in the form of bounteous catches. Tsutsui certainly hoped so since this was a make or break journey for him. He had been drafted in on a temporary basis when *The Lucky Dragon*'s regular skipper had to stay onshore for an operation. If the trip was a success with a good catch, it would cement Tsutsui's reputation as a reliable captain and help his career path. Fortunately the trawler had Yoshio Misaki amongst her crew who was considered to be one of the best fishing masters in the business.

Whilst the skipper is in charge of the day to day running of a tuna boat, the fishing master is the one who calls the shots when it comes to finding the fish. Whether or not a boat made good or meagre catches was down to his skill and experience. Misaki had the reputation of possessing a sixth sense when locating the shoals of tuna.

The fishing boat had been built in the classical style at the shipyard in Koza just up the coast. Originally designed to catch bonito fish, in 1953 she was converted to fish for the more profitable tuna. The boat was then bought by Kakuichi Nishikawa, a prominent local businessman who had been largely responsible for turning Yaizu into an important tuna fishing port.

It was his decision to change the vessel's name from *Kotoshiro-maru* to *The Lucky Dragon No 5*. In fact she was the fourth boat with this name, but Mr Nishikawa decided not to use the number four in the name since it is similar to the word death when spoken in Japanese. This would surely have brought ill-fortune on the vessel.

On this day, Kakuichi Nishikawa had boarded the boat for a confidential chat with Misaki as *The Lucky Dragon* prepared to set sail. Their discussion was about the all important business of finding the best fishing grounds. Whilst the crew believed they would be fishing in the waters around the Solomon Islands in the South Pacific, the two men had decided otherwise.

On this trip, *The Lucky Dragon* would be fishing around Midway Island at the western end of the Hawaiian Islands chain in the Northern Pacific. It was here that Nishikawa and Misaki decided the best albacore tuna shoals would be found. This had to be kept secret until the trawler was well away from port because Midway was not popular with crews. The area had a bad reputation for vicious storms and high seas. No fisherman likes to risk life and limb no matter how rich the catch. They did not know it at the time, but this secret decision by the owner and fishing master would change the lives of all aboard *The Lucky Dragon* forever.

At 11:30 in the morning, *The Lucky Dragon* finally departed on her journey into the Pacific. As she disappeared over the horizon the group of well wishers broke up to return to their homes. Unknown to them, the boat's departure was not as clean as they thought. A vital spare part for the diesel engine had inadvertently been left behind. This meant *The Lucky Dragon* had to put in to the neighbouring port of Ogawa so that the chief engineer Tadashi Yamamoto could ride back to Yaizu on a borrowed motorcycle to collect it.

Such a subterfuge was deemed necessary since returning to the home port so soon after leaving would not only involve loss of face but also be considered a very bad omen to the superstitious fishing community. As it was, the crew's woes were further compounded when *The Lucky Dragon* ran aground on entering the port. After one failed attempt to free her, she was lifted off by the early evening tide to continue her voyage. Everyone agreed this was not a good sign.

As if to confirm their fears, they ran into a terrible storm two days after leaving Japan which lasted for a further three days. On the same day that the storm lifted, the crew received the shocking news from Fishing Master Misaki. He informed them that their final destination was not the Solomon Islands in the South Pacific but Midway Island with its treacherous seas.

It must have been a tense meeting. The men were very angry and with good reason. Traditionally, crews were always kept informed about their vessel's fishing destination. In this instance, Misaki had flown in the face of convention, informing none of the crew including the Captain where they were going. The crewmen were also alarmed at the destination with some voicing fears that *The Lucky Dragon* would not survive the rough seas around Midway.

It took Misaki all his considerable strength of character and authority, but in the end he won the day. The fact that as fishing master, he was effectively in charge of the ship helped to sway the men. So, grumbling amongst themselves, they went along with his decision. On Wednesday January 27th 1954, *The Lucky Dragon* steered due east and sailed into the lonely vastness of the North Pacific. Eleven days later, on February 7th Misaki ordered the crew to fish for tuna in the seas around Midway.

Like all Japanese tuna boats at this time, *The Lucky Dragon* used the technique of long lining to catch fish. As its name suggests, this involved winching out a fishing line for long distances behind the boat. At intervals of about three hundred yards glass marker buoys floated on the surface attached by float line to the submerged long line. These had flags attached to bamboo poles and marked the points on the line where groups of one hundred baited hooks awaited their catch. At regular intervals buoys with battery powered lights were attached to mark the path of the line. This ensured it could easily be seen in darkness or poor light - an important factor since the boat's lines stretched for many miles behind the stern of the vessel.

Had things gone to plan, it is likely that *The Lucky Dragon* would have returned to Yaizu directly from Midway with a decent catch sometime in the middle of March. However, fate intervened in the shape of every fisherman's worst nightmare. On February 8th, about forty miles of fishing line was lost when it snagged on a coral outcrop.

Faced with the unwelcome prospect of returning empty handed to their home port, Misaki called the boat's decision makers together.

They included the captain, boatswain, chief engineer and radio operator. After a long discussion, the group decided to head due south to the Marshall Islands where the seas were calmer and the shoals of tuna more abundant.

Unfortunately, the seas around the North Western Marshall Islands yielded only modest catches. By 28th February 1954, *The Lucky Dragon* was eighty-five miles east of Bikini Atoll with only nine tons of tuna in her hold. Chief engineer Yamamoto was concerned they might not have enough fuel for the return journey. After conferring with Misaki, they agreed to throw the lines one last time on March 1st before heading home.

Whilst *The Lucky Dragon* was making her challenging journey, intensive final preparations for a world shattering event were reaching their conclusion on the isolated atoll of Bikini in the U.S. administered Marshall Islands. This remote but beautiful outcrop of palms, sand and coral had been selected in 1946 for the testing of America's nuclear arsenal.

These days, pulverising and contaminating an island paradise seems nothing less than an outrageous act of state vandalism. The mid 1950s were different and dangerous times. Barely a year before, The Korean War pitting North Korea and the Communist Powers against the American led U.N. Forces had ended in the stalemate of a ceasefire. This state of frozen war would last for the next seven decades.

The Cold War between the United States and the Soviet Union was also at ts height with both sides racing to create larger and better weapons of mass destruction.

The Americans were currently ahead of their communist rivals with their new H-bomb. It was many times more powerful than the atomic bombs dropped on Hiroshima and Nagasaki, but it needed testing and Bikini Atoll, way out in the middle of the Pacific had been chosen for this doubtful privilege. The atoll had already been the site of a series of tests codenamed *Operation Crossroads*.

Now a new dry fuel thermonuclear hydrogen bomb was due to be tested on Bikini at dawn on March 1st 1954. It would be the first of three such tests Codenamed *Castle Bravo*.

By the early morning hours of February 28th 1954, *The Lucky Dragon* was situated just outside the 57,000 square mile U.S. Exclusion Zone (Danger Zone) surrounding the Bikini Atoll test area. At about one a.m. the crew of the tuna boat threw their lines for the last time.

Captain Tsutsui and the crew were aware they were close to the American nuclear test area. Indeed, Aikichi Kuboyama, the trawler's radio operator warned the captain and the fishing master to specifically avoid Bikini as this was where the Americans had been detonating their nuclear weapons. However, Captain Tsutsui and fishing master Misaki believed there had been no testing on Bikini since 1946. This was because in 1952, the Japanese Maritime Safety Board identified Eniwetok Atoll 600 miles from their current position as the existing nuclear test area.

Since *The Lucky Dragon* was so close to the actual site of the *Castle Bravo* test it seems strange they were not spotted by any aerial patrols along the perimeter of the exclusion zone. Indeed, the question must be asked if the U.S. authorities suspended these patrols for some reason. All the crew, particularly Kuboyama, the radio operator were adamant that they received no radio warnings nor observed any surveillance aircraft whilst they were in the vicinity of Bikini Atoll.

At dawn on that fateful March day, the crew were awakened by a truly strange event. Apparently, the sun was rising in the West! Due to the early hour, only a few of the crew actually witnessed the phenomenon. One was Yoshio Misaki, the fishing master who was on the bridge calculating the trawler's position with his sextant. Another, was Shinzo Suzuki who was on deck because he could not sleep.

In his book *The Voyage of The Lucky Dragon,* Ralph E. Lapp vividly describes what Suzuki saw on that humid spring morning:

"*Suddenly, the skies in the west lighted up and a great flare of whitish yellow light splashed against the clouds and illuminated the water.*"

Although he was shocked by the bizarre sight, Fishing Master Misaki had the presence of mind to note the time and direction of the huge flash. By now, many of the crew had come on deck to witness the spectacle. Chattering excitedly amongst themselves, the men speculated what it might be. With the A-bombs of Hiroshima and Nagasaki still fresh in their collective memory, more than one thought it could be a nuclear explosion. Whatever the cause, the majority including Misaki felt it was a bad omen.

Seven minutes later, the vessel was enveloped in a huge sound wave that seemed to come from all directions. After recovering from their shock and fear, Fishing Master Misaki with Captain Tsutsui had a quick conference about what to do. Their immediate reaction was to simply cut the fishing lines and run for safety, but the thought of losing the rest of their lines and the valuable remainder of their catch was too much.

In the end they decided to haul the lines in. The trawler had been hit by the concussive blast seven minutes after the flash which was in the direction of Bikini Atoll. According to Kuboyama, the radio operator, that was where the Americans were exploding their nuclear bombs.

By his calculations, with the speed of sound being 1000 feet a second, they were only 85 miles from the nuclear explosion, if that's what it was. This calculation also closely matched Misaki's sextant reading at 87 miles. Kuboyama's instinct was to get as far away from the area as soon as possible and sadly he would be proved right. Tadashi Yamamoto, the chief engineer, who had been against the decision to fish in this area all along certainly agreed.

While the laborious business of hauling in the lines continued, darkness turned to daylight only for the clear skies to rapidly darken with storm clouds. A short while later, fine white ash rained down on their boat for about three hours. One crew member, Matashichi Oishi even tasted some of the ash and found it gritty and flavourless. Others like Kuboyama the radio operator also tasted the ash but he found it salty. One or two of the men kept samples of the dust in folds of paper.

As *The Lucky Dragon* began the 2,300 mile journey back home on March 2nd, crew members began complaining about irritations to their eyes. The dust also stuck to their skin and hair causing acute discomfort. In the days that followed these symptoms were compounded by skin abrasions, loss of appetite, nausea and diarrhoea. What the fisherman could not know at the time is that they were suffering from acute radiation syndrome (A.R.S.).

This had come from the largest nuclear blast in history making the crew the first ever victims of an H-bomb. Due to a miscalculation by the scientists involved, the *Castle Bravo* bomb on Bikini was considerably more powerful than they estimated. Instead of a blast of 6 to 8 megatons it yielded an explosion of 15 megatons which was a thousand times greater than the bombs dropped on Japan.

Unlike those two A-bombs, *Castle Bravo* was not detonated in the air but from a tower just 150 feet above the ground. As a result, a far larger amount of radioactive debris was sucked thousands of feet into the sky. This finally fell back to earth covering the surrounding area including the inhabited islands of Rongerik, Rongelap and Uterik Atolls with radioactive debris.

The whole of Rongelap was blanketed by nearly an inch of highly radioactive calcium ash giving it the unreal appearance of a heavy snowfall.

By the time they were evacuated by U.S, forces two days later, the whole population were suffering from acute radiation sickness or syndrome. Symptoms included burning eyes, vomiting, diarrhoea and swollen limbs. The inhabitants of the two other islands were also suffering from A.R.S.

After a long and difficult journey, *The Lucky Dragon* finally arrived back in Yaizu Port at 5:30 a.m on Sunday March 14th. It would not prove to be an easy homecoming for the crew or their families. Apart from the other symptoms such as nausea and skin lesions, most of the crew had developed extremely dark complexions. It was as if they had been burned black.

Initial inspections of the crew by a local physician, Doctor Oi, left him baffled. Like most of the Japanese medical community, he had some knowledge of radiation because of Hiroshima and Nagasaki, but the full extent of the men's condition was a mystery to him. Two of the crew Sanjiro Masuda and and Tadashi Yamamoto, volunteered to go to the Tokyo University Hospital the next day for a more complete examination. Eventually, they would be followed by the rest of the crew who would spend long months in isolation away from their families.

In the meantime, *The Lucky Dragon's* tuna catch was removed and sent for sale at the large fish market in Osaka. With the benefit of hindsight this may seem strange, but the fish were not considered to be seriously contaminated since they had been stored below decks. It was also important for both the owner and crew to recoup as much as possible from the disastrous voyage. Nevertheless this would have far reaching consequences as the story of the Bikini Fishermen eventually broke.

This happened on the following Tuesday March 16th with a front page headline on the *Yomiuri* newspaper informing a shocked world that Japanese fisherman had been contaminated by an American nuclear blast. From then on all hell broke loose with the 23 fishermen finding themselves and their chances of survival a matter of very public concern. There was a great deal of wild speculation in the newspapers and on television about the health and the ultimate fate of the fishermen. This period was also marked by a significant low in the relationship between the American and Japanese governments.

Osaka biophysicist Yasushi Nishiwaki and his American born wife Jane became involved in *The Lucky Dragon* saga as soon as the story broke in the press. As a specialist in the study of radioactivity, the incident immediately caught Yasushi's attention. Shortly afterwards, he went down the tuna from Yaizu.

Some doctors were already on site and their geiger counters registered only a low radiation reading from the fish. Nishiwaki's more sensitive equipment told a very different story. Whilst he could not be sure without further analysis, his readings indicated that the Yaizu tuna were highly radioactive. With Nishiwaki's geiger counters clicking away frenetically every time they were held close to the tuna, it was not long before they earned the sinister nickname of *Crying Fish.* Whilst the radioactive tuna from the market were hastily buried, some had already been sold on.

News of the contaminated fish in Osaka spread far and fast causing a total collapse in the sales of fish, one of Japan's staple food sources. Following their visit to the fish market, the Nishiwakis travelled down to Yaizu to check out *The Lucky Dragon* and her crew members for radiation. In the event, both yielded high levels of radiation. The Nishiwakis found this to be baffling and alarming.

Whilst Nishiwaki's knowledge of radiation was as extensive as anyone's it was still largely based on the Hiroshima and Nagasaki bombs. Although devastating in the effect of their blasts, these yielded only small amounts of radioactive fallout covering a relatively limited geographical area.

This was because the Hiroshima and Nagasaki bombs had detonated in the air and had not sucked up a significant amount of debris and dust from the ground. As a result, the spread of radioactive contamination had been limited to a small area around the actual targets. In the case of the Bikini Atoll bomb, it seemed the fishermen had been contaminated a considerable distance from the blast. This was totally new and uncharted territory for the young physicist.

To find out the precise nature of the radiation he was dealing with Nishiwaki needed information on the fissile materials that made up the *Castle Bravo* H-bomb. Until the Japanese medical specialists had this, they would have no idea how to treat *The Lucky Dragon* fishermen. Only the American Government could provide that crucial information.

The problem was that Nishiwaki had no idea who to contact in the U.S. Atomic Energy Commission for this information. So he decided the best way was to send an open letter to the U.S. authorities via an American press service in Tokyo. He waited in vain for a reply. The reason for this was that the journalist with whom he had entrusted the letter never sent it. Apparently, this was because the American reporter believed Nishiwaki was nothing more than an attention seeking alarmist and that the radioactivity story had little or no substance.

The official U.S. Government announcement of the *Castle Bravo* blast and the subsequent accidental contamination of some of their own people as well as local inhabitants was contained in this very low key statement:

During the course of a routine atomic test in the Marshall Islands, 28 United States personnel and 236 residents were transported from neighbouring atolls to Kwajalein Island according to plans as a precautionary measure.

The individuals were unexpectedly exposed to some radiation. There were no burns. All are reported well. After completion of the atomic tests, they will be returned to their homes. **(1)**

Once the story of *The Lucky Dragon's* ill fated voyage and the plight of her crew broke, it caused a worldwide media firestorm. In the furore that followed, the U.S. Government went into panic mode insisting that the crew of *The Lucky Dragon* had not been affected by radiation at all. Initially, the head of the Atomic Energy Commission inferred that the burns on the fishermen's bodies had been caused by burnt lime which is created when coral is calcined.

When it soon became clear this was nonsense, the authorities claimed incorrectly that not only was *The Lucky Dragon* inside the exclusion zone but it could well have been a Soviet plant designed to embarrass the U.S. Government. They also insisted that the contamination was much less serious than it actually was. The U.S. Food & Drug Administration was taking no chances however and placed strict restrictions on the importation of tuna. As a nine year old boy over in England, I well remember my mother doing her bit by throwing out all the tinned crab and and tuna in our larder.

"I'm not even feeding this to the cats," she insisted.

It was about his time that the emotive phrase *She No Hai* (*Ashes of Death* in English) began to appear in the press. This was the name given to the ash that had showered down on The *Lucky Dragon* and her crew for several hours after the explosion. It is self evident from the name that the media already suspected this ash was from the nuclear blast. What everyone wanted, was confirmation of this from the U.S. authorities.

It is fair to say that probably due to constraints of national security, the Americans were less than forthcoming than they could have been. On three occasions various U.S. representatives failed to answer this crucial question posed by Japanese scientists and doctors: *Had the Lucky Dragon and her crew been irradiated by an H-Bomb?* The closest to an answer came from Dr Merrill Eisenbud, Director of the A.E.C.'s Health & Safety Laboratory. He referred the doctors and scientists to Dr Kimura of the Institute of Scientific Research in Tokyo. (2)

To cut a long and involved story short, Dr Kimura was Japan's leading radio physicist. In 1938, he led a team which managed to split particles of Uranium 238 and Uranium 235 to create a new species of Uranium they called U 237. At the time, this experimentation was done in the spirit of pure scientific research.

When the Americans also succeeded in splitting U 238 and U 235 a few years later it was to create the big brother of the atomic bomb, the H-bomb. Dr Kimura and his team had analysed some of the ash particles collected by *The Lucky Dragon* crew and discovered they contained significant amounts of U 237. Circumstantially, this gave them the answer to their quest that the device exploded by the Americans at Bikini Atoll on 1st March 1954 was indeed a new species of nuclear weapon with unlimited power.

So what eventually happened to those twenty-three Japanese tuna fisherman?

All but one of the crew members survived and of those, only one ever returned to sea again. He was Yamamoto, the chief engineer who had managed to find work on a training ship.

After recovering from their ordeal in May 1955, the former fishermen moved into a variety of land based jobs and enterprises. For example, Susumu Mizaki (no relation to the fishing master) opened a shop selling tofu, a soya milk based delicacy much prized by the Japanese. Whilst the former cook of *The Lucky Dragon* Takeiji Hattori found employment in a local ironworks.

Matashichi Oishi, the twenty year old fisherman who tasted the radioactive ash, set up a dry cleaning business in a different town to Yaizu. In the 1980s he also made positive use of the traumatic experience of that fated voyage by giving lectures advocating nuclear disarmament. In 2011 he published a book about his experiences called *The Day the Sun Rose in The West. The Lucky Dragon and I.*

Miraculously, none of the crew members had suffered the fate they all had feared of being made infertile by the radiation. More importantly, a number had got married and produced healthy children.

Sadly, Aikichi Kuboyama, the trawler's much loved and respected radio operator was not so lucky. He became the only fatality of *The Lucky Dragon* tragedy. Whilst being treated in hospital for the effects of the radiation his condition sharply deteriorated in August 1954. He was never to recover and died on 23rd September. He left a widow and three young daughters.

His funeral service in Yaizu on 9th October was attended by 3,000 people including 200 students from Shizouka University who sang a lament called *A Bomb Never Forgiven*.

At least the press coverage brought some small benefit to *The Lucky Dragon's* crew and their families by way of compensation. The U.S. Government paid the widow of Aikichi Kuboyama approximately $2,800 ($26,100 in 2021 values). Separately, the U.S. Government paid the Japanese Government $15,300,000 compensation from which the fishery where *The Lucky Dragon* operated received $2,000,000. From this sum each surviving crewman received $5,550, worth $51,800 in 2021 values. However, this money could only go so far in alleviating the suffering these victims had endured.

To compound their problems, during their treatment for the acute radiation sickness the crew received blood transfusions that were contaminated with hepatitis C.

If this were not bad enough, they and their families were also stigmatised because of their radiation sickness. This was sadly common in Japan at this time where it was erroneously believed that radiation sickness was contagious. Previously it was the *hibakusha,* as the survivors of the Hiroshima and Nagasaki bombs were known, who bore the brunt of this irrational prejudice.

The actual tuna fishing boat, *The Lucky Dragon,* was safely decontaminated and in 1976 was placed in an exhibition hall dedicated to the incident in Tokyo.

As for the unfortunate inhabitants of those contaminated atolls in the Marshall Islands, they were dealt a very raw deal. The islanders of Bikini Atoll evacuated their island in 1946 on the understanding from the U.S. authorities this was temporary and they would be able to return after the testing programme had finished.

They were relocated to Rongerik 125 miles to the east which was not only one sixth the size of Bikini but was also unsuited to the subsistence farming the islanders were used to. This was because the local water supplies were inadequate and soil was insufficiently fertile. Although the Americans left them with some food supplies these ran out within a few weeks. After that, it seems the Bikinians were forgotten by the authorities. The result of this official indifference was that they were left to slowly *"starve to death"* as columnist Harold Ickes put it.

He was not alone in this assessment. Dr. Leonard E. Mason, an anthropologist from the University of Hawaii, visited the relocated islanders on Rongerik Atoll and was horrified when he found they were actually starving. Since that time, the Bikinians were relocated to other atolls eventually making the island of Kili their permanent home. In 1987, there was a failed attempt by islanders to return to live on Bikini itself. This project eventually had to be abandoned because the water and staple food sources such as coconut crabs on the atoll were too contaminated with radiation for safe permanent habitation.

Following the *Castle Bravo* test in 1954, inhabitants of Rongerik, Rongelap and Uterik Atolls were also hurriedly evacuated with only the clothes they stood up in. They were placed on other smaller islands as a 'temporary measure.' In virtually all cases this soon became permanent with few if any of the islanders ever seeing their homes or belongings again.

Since 1975, The United States Government has provided the dispossessed Marshallese islanders compensation of approximately $150,000,000. Whilst this provided material comfort, nothing could compensate for the loss of traditional lifestyle and ancestral lands caused by the radiation from the nuclear tests.

There is also the issue of many severe ongoing health problems that have dogged past, present and future generations of Marshall Islanders due to the radiation from the tests. These include high rates of leukaemia, thyroid and lung cancer. Cervical cancer rates in the female population of the Marshall Islands are sixty times higher than in the United States.

Whilst Bikini and other atolls that bore the brunt of the high radiation have proved to be uninhabitable for humans it is a different story for the marine life. The fish and crabs have proved to be surprisingly resilient to the radiation. In 2017, Steve Palumbi a marine biologist from Stanford University led a study team to Bikini Atoll. They reported seeing the lagoon teeming with shoals of fish including large numbers of nurse sharks. The coral also appeared healthy with a significant population of coconut crabs. The team also found very few deformities amongst these animals caused by the radiation.

The fact that the hydrogen bomb, an agent of mass destruction has been responsible for creating this sanctuary for such a diverse marine ecosystem is indeed a sad irony.

The detonation of the *Castle Bravo* bomb on Bikini Atoll led to the worst case of radioactive contamination in U.S. history. Radioactive particles were spread over an area of 4,200 square miles. This, coupled with *The Lucky Dragon* contamination and a Soviet nuclear test spreading radioactive fallout in Japan, caused a sharp rise in international concern over atmospheric pollution of above ground nuclear tests.

In 1954 Indian Prime Minister Jawarhalal Nehru became the first world leader to call for a moratorium on the testing of nuclear weapons. In the same year the British Labour Party led by Clement Attlee also called for a nuclear test ban. Early in 1955 Soviet President Nikita Kruschev proposed talks with the aim of banning atmospheric tests.

This was the start of the long journey to ban these tests. Its culmination was The Partial Test Ban Treaty which was signed in Moscow on 5th August 1963 by the U.S., Soviet and British governments.

With the signing of this treaty, the three post war powers probably thought they had contained the nuclear genie in a bottle of their choosing. Worryingly, in the intervening decades, the number of countries that are now nuclear powers has grown steadily. Today the Nuclear Club has no less than nine states including France, China, India, Pakistan, North Korea and Israel (probably), United Kingdom, U.S. and Russia. Iran could well become the tenth member of this club within the next decade.

It is to be hoped that even the most unpredictable of these nuclear powers such as North Korea will be constrained from using these dreadful weapons by the doctrine of Mutually Assured Destruction. MAD indeed.

Sources

Voyage of The Lucky Dragon by Ralph E. Lapp Penguin Books 1957)

(1) *Page 55 Voyage of The Lucky Dragon by Ralph E. Lapp Penguin Books 1957.*

(2) *Page 133 Voyage of The Lucky Dragon.*

Bikini Atoll as it is today. It has 4-6 caretakers living there including Edward Maddison a grandson of one of the original inhabitants. Bikini is a UNESCO World Heritage site and listed as Bikini Atoll Nuclear Test Site.

Photograph by Ron Van Oers - Wikimedia

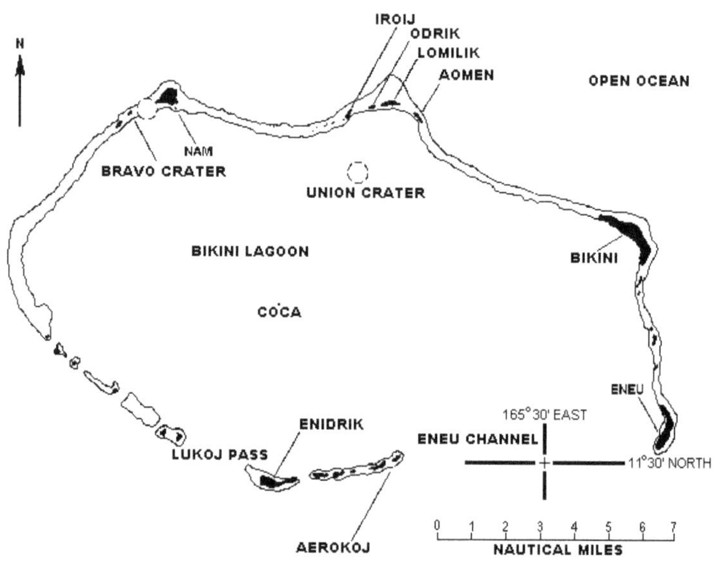

Map of Bikini Atoll showing the location of The Castle Bravo Explosion at top left hand point on the coral reef.

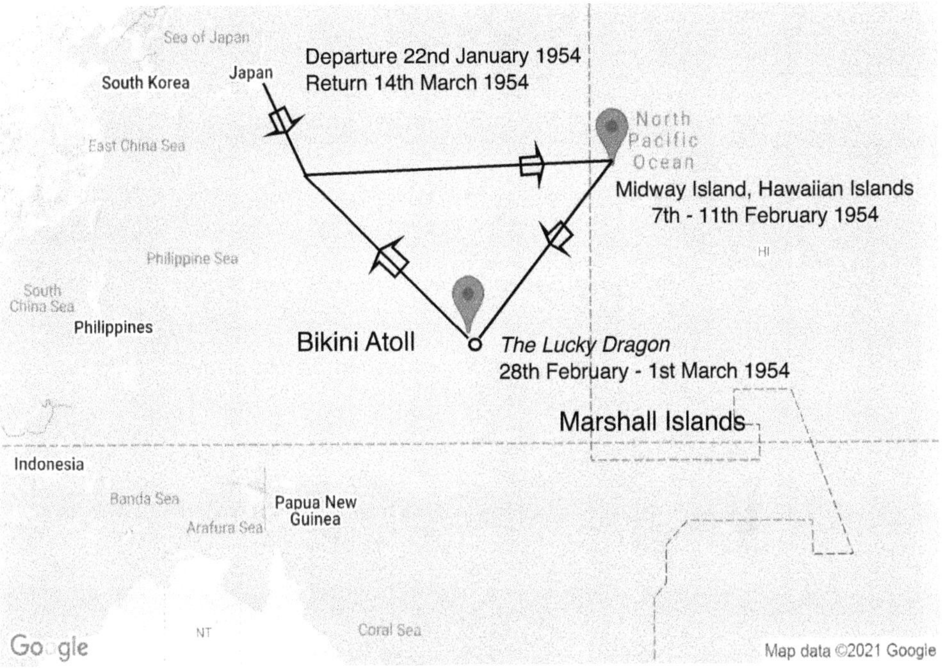

Sea of Japan
Departure 22nd January 1954
Return 14th March 1954
South Korea
Japan
East China Sea
North Pacific Ocean
Midway Island, Hawaiian Islands
7th - 11th February 1954
HI
Philippine Sea
South China Sea
Philippines
Bikini Atoll
The Lucky Dragon
28th February - 1st March 1954
Marshall Islands
Indonesia
Banda Sea
Arafura Sea
Papua New Guinea
NT
Coral Sea
Google
Map data ©2021 Google

Map showing *The Lucky Dragon* tuna fishing boat's final journey 22nd January - 14th March 1954

Maps created by N Brazil using Google template.

Bikini Atoll
Ist March 1954
The Lucky Dragon
28th February - 1st March 1954
Federated States of Micronesia
Marshall Islands
Ajeltake
Bikenibeu
Google
Map data ©2021

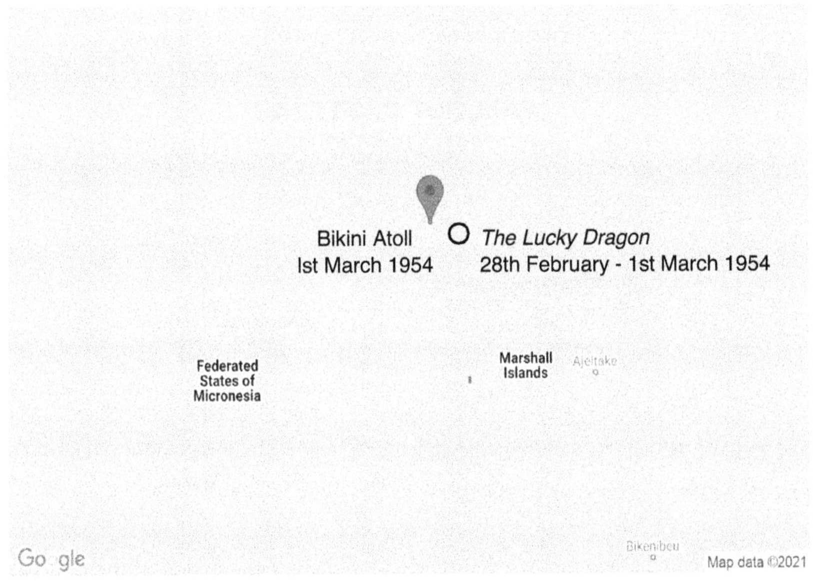

Map showing approximate position of *The Lucky Dragon* at the time of the Castle Bravo Explosion on Bikini Atoll 1st March 1954

The Castle Bravo Explosion
1st March 1954
Photograph: Dept of Energy/US Government

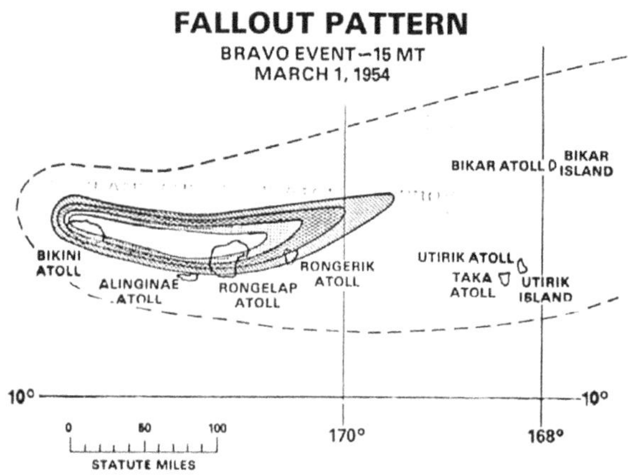

This map by US Department of Energy gives an idea of the extent of the radioactive plume from the Castle Bravo Test on 1st March 1954.
Image: Departmery of Energy/US Government

The Lucky Dragon Number Five tuna fishing boat and crew shortly before her last fateful voyage.
Photograph: Anonymous

Inhabitants leaving Bikini Atoll 7th March 1946. Despite promises by US Government, they would never return.
Photograph courtesy United States Navy

Chapter 4
The Most Polluted Place on Earth
The Kyshtym and Mayak Nuclear Disasters
Urals, Soviet Union
29th September 1957

Very few people know about the Russian city of Ozersk and with good reason. For it owes its existence to that dark and secret period of the 20th Century known as the Cold War.

In 1947, Stalin was desperate to catch up with the Americans in the nuclear arms race. To this end he ordered the establishment of a top secret plant to create weapons grade uranium and plutonium deep in the Eastern Urals 1,300 kilometres from Moscow. It was called Mayak which is the Russian word for lighthouse. Why it was given such a nautical name when it is so far from the sea is anybody's guess. Perhaps that was the point, to throw Russia's enemies off the scent.

In the same year a city was built with slave labour next to the plant. This was to accommodate the workers and scientists who were employed at Mayak. It was one of many such closed cities built to house the workers at similar nuclear plants that were dotted across the Soviet Union. Their existence was so secret that they did not appear on any maps. Mayak's city did not even have its own name and was originally called Chelyabinsk 40 after the nearest large city 55 miles away. The number 40 referred to the post office in Chelyabinsk through which all mail for the closed city was channelled. It was only in 1994 with the freedoms brought by *perestroika* that it became known as Ozersk.

Mayak was the birthplace of the Russian nuclear weapons programme. It was here that Igor Kurchatov 'the father of the Soviet Atomic bomb' developed that country's weapons of mass destruction. Situated on the shores of a beautiful lake called Irtyash, Chelyabinsk 40 was a dream city for its inhabitants surrounded by miles of beautiful forests and lakes. Unlike millions of their fellow countrymen and women the citizens of Chelyabinsk 40 lacked for nothing in facilities such as schools and restaurants. Supplies of food, groceries and commodities like soap were also plentiful. This was an unheard of state of affairs in the rest of the Soviet Union.

Appropriately, the Soviet nuclear weapons programme was overseen by Lavrentiy Beria, Stalin's feared head of secret police. Once inside its barbed wire boundary the secret city was a gilded prison for its inhabitants and almost impossible to leave except in special circumstances.

If any of the inhabitants paid a rare visit to family or friends on the outside, they were forbidden to mention where they actually lived. If asked, they would just say they lived on Lenin Street in the regional capital of Chelyabinsk. It was also drummed into their children that if they ever revealed their true home they would be taken away and shot.

Like its American counterpart, the Soviet Nuclear weapons programme had top priority. Working conditions at Soviet weapons plants such as Mayak were very unsafe with little regard for the health or wellbeing of its workers. Inevitably this led to corners being cut making the whole programme a disaster waiting to happen. It is fair to point out that such safety lapses in state nuclear programmes are not limited to Russia. There have also been bad safety lapses in both the British and American programmes as shown in subsequent chapters in this book.

Production of plutonium at the Mayak plant created a large amount of radioactive waste. This was placed in subterranean water store facilities situated beneath the plant itself. When these storage tanks were filled up the management did not halt production of the plutonium until additional tanks were constructed. Instead, between 1949 and 1951 they dumped large amounts of radioactive waste into the nearby Techa river.

This radioactive waste was then carried downstream to pollute a vast area of swampland and lakes. A total of 124,000 people who used the river in this area for fishing, washing, bathing and irrigation were also subjected to sustained levels of high radiation.

Inevitably, many people became sick, exhibiting all the classic symptoms of radiation sickness including fatigue, weight loss, low fertility and birth defects. Even in a highly secretive and paranoid state like the Soviet Union, this could not be ignored. Over the next decade 22 villages were evacuated and destroyed.

For some reason, perhaps because of logistical difficulties, this did not include the largest community of Muslumovo. Instead the village became a living laboratory with the people being checked for their general health and radiation levels on an annual basis.

Even today, nearly 30 years after the end of the Soviet Union, Ozersk remains a closed city with many dark secrets. This would have remained the case indefinitely were it not for the courage of Samira Goetschal an Iranian/American film maker who made a remarkable documentary about the city in 2016. Called simply *City 40*, it was shot in secret within Ozersk with the co-operation of some of its citizens who felt compelled to speak out.

The film shows a place that, on the face of it, is remarkably pleasant and normal. Children can be seen skateboarding in public parks whilst young mothers push their babies in buggies and prams. It also reveals sinister truths about the city by showing the graves of many young people aged 18 to 35 buried in the city's Birch Grove Cemetery who have died and continue to die from radiation poisoning. It also covers the dramatic events of 29th September 1957 which had a profound effect on a large area of the Urals and its inhabitants.

Sometime in that year, one of the coolers surrounding the tanks holding all that highly radioactive waste beneath the Mayak plant failed. For some reason, probably simple neglect, the cooler was not repaired. These coolers were necessary since all such radioactive waste heats up as it decays. If the heat generated by this process is not controlled it will eventually explode.

The absence of the cooler left the 80 tons of nuclear waste in the container to heat up unchecked. Early in the evening of 29th September 1957 this heating passed the critical point of 350 degrees centigrade and a massive explosion occurred. The 160 ton concrete lid of the waste container was flung high into the air.

The explosion released a huge concentration of radioactive particles that were carried by the wind in a north easterly direction. The radiation cloud eventually reached 350 kilometres beyond Mayak.

The deadly invisible plume contaminated an area of the Urals measuring approximately 24,000 square kilometres (9,000 square miles) and expose its 470,000 inhabitants to high levels of radiation. This radiological event would become known as The East Urals Radioactive Trace (EURT). The precise area of contamination is difficult to assess because of the secrecy surrounding everything related to Mayak and the accident. For the same reason, the death toll for this release remained unclear until 1989 with estimates ranging from 66 to over 8,000 people.

In spite of strenuous efforts by the Soviet authorities to keep the accident secret, some sketchy reports of a major accident began to appear in the western media. In 1959, *Die Presse*, an Austrian newspaper gave a more detailed account of the disaster. Two years later, the CIA obtained aerial photographs of the damaged area spreading from Mayak to the North East using their U2 spy planes.

The Soviets would continue to deny that an accident happened. Then in 1976, dissident Russian scientist Zhores Medvedev wrote his detailed account of the accident in *The New Scientist* magazine. In the article, Medvedev strongly criticised the authorities for the method of nuclear waste disposal:

"Nuclear scientists had often warned about the dangers involved in this primitive method of waste disposal, but nobody listened. Suddenly there was an enormous explosion. The nuclear reactions had led to overheating in the burial grounds. The explosion poured radioactive materials high into the sky. It was just the wrong weather for such a tragedy. Strong winds blew the radioactive clouds hundreds of miles away. Tens of thousands of people were affected, hundreds dying, though the real figures have never been made public."

Medvedev always insisted that the numbers who died as a result of the accident were in the thousands. Initially, his account of the accident was dismissed by many scientific sources. Surprisingly many of these were not from Russia but in the West.

Some of the attacks were both fanciful and vitriolic. Medvedev later related how British and American scientists accused him of being everything from an outright charlatan to a KGB agent and anti-nuclear scaremonger. It seems quite extraordinary that one of Russia's leading dissidents who had been incarcerated in a mental hospital to shut him up should have his reputation impugned in this way.

However his account of the disaster was soon corroborated by Professor Lev Tumerman formerly of the Engelhard Institute of Molecular Biology in Moscow.

It was at this time that I remember hearing Professor Tumerman being interviewed on the BBC Radio 4 Today programme. In it he described travelling through an extensive area near to Mayak which was effectively a radioactive dead zone because of the accident. His vehicle had to travel at speed and it was forbidden to stop. He and his colleagues were not allowed to drink any of the local water.

In 1989, the Soviet authorities finally admitted there had been a nuclear disaster in the Urals. In a report to the the International Atomic Energy Agency (IAEA) in Vienna, they said that the accident had led to three regions: Chelyabinsk, Sverdlovsk and Tumen being contaminated with radioactivity.

Boris Vasileyvich Nikipelov, the First Deputy Minister for Machine Building said the accident had been due to an inadequate knowledge of *"the effects of temperature"* on decaying nuclear waste. He also blamed *"certain operational violations"*. In other words, human error had also played a part. (*New Scientist 5th August 1989*). The Soviet authorities continued to insist there had been no fatalities.

It was not until after the collapse of the Soviet Union that official confirmation of the extent of the Kyshtym Disaster became known. In June 1992 the Russian Institute of Biophysics, a part of the Russian Ministry of Health, released a report which stated that: Since 1949, *'no less than 150 million curies (5.1018 becquerels) of radioactive substances have been discharged into the environment as a result of Mayak's activities'*. By comparison, the Chernobyl disaster released 50 million curies of radioactivity.

The report also confirmed that between 1949 and 1956, 76 million cubic litres of radioactive waste was poured into the lakes and rivers surrounding the Mayak plant. According to the report 124,000 people who relied on these water sources for drinking were at risk of radiation poisoning. The report concluded that in the 32 years following the disaster, 8015 people had died as a result of radioactive contamination. (*Source: New Scientist 20th June 1992*).

This was a disregard for human life on an epic scale.

To date, the Kyshtym Disaster (Named after the nearest big town) remains the third worst nuclear disaster after Fukushima and Chernobyl. Both of these are at the highest rating of Level 7 on the International Nuclear Event Scale (INES). Kyshtym is one below this at Level 6.

The Mayak Plant is no longer used for the production of plutonium for nuclear weapons. It now specialises in reprocessing nuclear waste. Quite how this is working out is difficult to assess since its operations are still largely secret.

From its inception to the present day, Mayak has had a poor safety record with a litany of over thirty major and smaller nuclear incidents. As well as the Kyshtym Disaster in September 1957, a major radiation leak occurred ten years later. In this incident, Lake Karachay near the plant that had been used as a dumping ground for nuclear waste had dried up. In 1967, winds scattered the radioactive dust from the lake bed over Ozersk irradiating 400,000 inhabitants.

In the Autumn of 2017, a noticeable increase in radioactivity was recorded in central Europe. The suspected source was Mayak, although the Russian authorities denied there had been any incident. However, the Russians did admit to measuring abnormally high levels of radioactivity in village of Argyash ten miles to the south of the Mayak plant.

In 1968 part of the area known as the East Urals Radioactive Trace which was contaminated as a result of the 1957 accident was re-designated as The East Urals Nature Reserve. This was to prohibit public access and disguise the extent of the radiation in the area. It is thought to be still uninhabitable today and likely to remain that way for the foreseeable future.

Sources

City 40 - Documentary directed by Samira Goetschal about Ozersk & Mayak 2016 (Available on Netflix)
Mayak Half Life - Greenpeace documentary about Mayak and Muslumovo village 2002 (Available on You Tube)
Zhores Medvedev - New Scientist Article 1956
Nuclear Disaster In The Urals By Zhores Medvedev
Published by W W Norton & Co 1980
Soviet Union comes clean on nuclear blast. New Scientist 5/08/1989
By Judith Perera And Roger Milne
Kyshtym 'almost as bad as Chernobyl' New Scientist 23/12/1989
By David Dickson
Soviet plutonium plant 'killed thousands' New Scientist 20/06/1992
By Judith Perera
Russia's toxic shocker - Bomb factories created the most radioactive place on Earth New Scientist 6/12/97
By Rob Edwards
Russia Starts Crash Nuclear Power Programme New Scientist 23/01/93
By Debora MacKenzie
Exposed: Soviet cover-up of nuclear fallout worse than Chernobyl New Scientist 20/03/2017 By Fred Pearce

Two Maps showing the geographical position of Mayak and the closed city of Ozersk in relation to Europe and to Chelyabinsk, one of the nearest main cities to the plant and where all the post for Ozersk, where Mayak's workers lived, was routed.

In 1968 the most contaminated area from the 1957 disaster was declared the East Urals '*Zapovednik*' (Strict Nature Reserve). This sign warns that public entry is forbidden.
Photograph courtesy Ecodefense/Heinrich Boell Stiftung Russia/Slapovskaya/Nikulina via Wikipedia

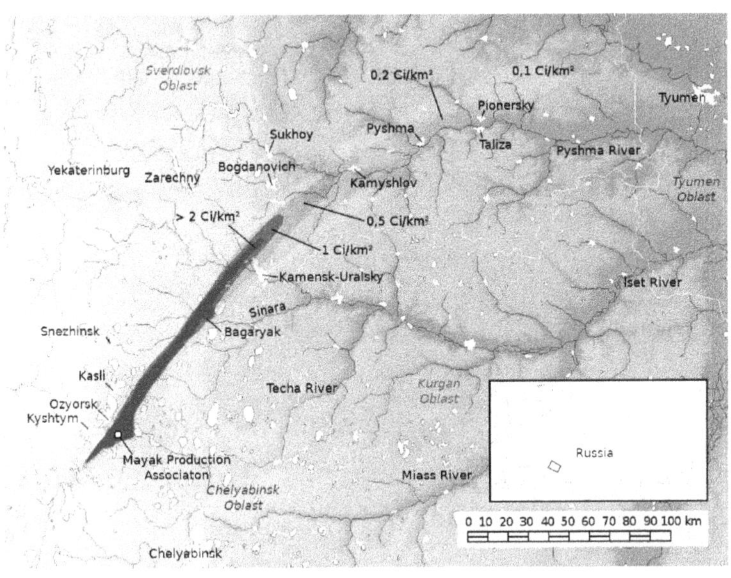

Map shows the extent of the radioactive contamination caused by the 1957 Mayak nuclear disaster. Now known as The East Urals Radiation Trace.
Map by Goran tek-en, Jan Rieke, maps-for-free.com, NordNordWest, Historicair, Bourrichon, Insider, Kneiphof via Wikipedia

Chapter 5
The Forty Year Contamination
Rocky Flats Nuclear Plant, Denver, Colorado, U.S.
11th September 1957 & 11th May 1969

In the early 1950s, the U.S. Atomic Energy Commission needed a plant to manufacture plutonium 'trigger' cores for America's growing arsenal of nuclear weapons. They finally settled on a site tucked away on a windy rock strewn plateau in the mountainous country fifteen miles to the northwest of the city of Denver, Colorado. The original site covered an area of 2,519 acres.

The plant that was built there took its name from the area - Rocky Flats. From 1952 until its closure in 1992, it manufactured its deadly products in conditions of utmost secrecy. When work first started on the plant in 1951, the government insisted the facility would *not* manufacture nuclear bombs.

However, the authorities conceded that the Rocky Flats Plant might be used to make plutonium and uranium components for such weapons. It says much about the public mindset in the 1950s that the large majority of the local population took the government at its word on this.

In fact, from the start, the primary role of The Rocky Flats Plant was to manufacture plutonium cores for nuclear bombs. About the size and shape of a grapefruit, these cores (also known as pits) are the triggers that start the explosive chain reaction when a nuclear bomb is dropped in anger. In other words, they are the heart of atomic and hydrogen bombs. The U.S. Government knew this of course as did all the official bodies involved, but the general public were consistently misled and kept in the dark about the Rocky Flats Plant's deadly secret.

In 1974 a further 4,027 acres was added to the site for plant expansion. The company that the U.S. Government chose to run the plant was The Dow Chemical Company. During its forty year life, Rocky Flats Plant experienced three major radiation accidents that also affected the surrounding areas including the city of Denver itself. As well as these three large accidents, there were also legions of smaller fires, accidents and leaks that are too numerous to include here. The cumulative effect of all these incidents was a steady build-up of radioactive contamination in the area surrounding the plant. For many years, the various government agencies and the plant management insisted both the facility itself and the surrounding area was completely safe.

The first serious incident was a major fire on 11th September 1957. It broke out at 10 p.m. in what was known as one of the plant's glove boxes. These sealed containers with built in protective gloves are used for the handling of hazardous materials. A production line of these glove boxes was housed in Building 71 for the purpose of manufacturing the plutonium cores. Inside the glove boxes the plutonium cores were milled into shape. Inevitably, plutonium shavings from this process would drop to the base of the boxes.

The fire occurred. when some of these shavings of highly radioactive plutonium within one of these glove boxes spontaneously ignited. This is not as strange as it sounds since plutonium is pyrophoric meaning it can spontaneously combust in contact with the air.

The fire spread rapidly through a succession of glove boxes on the production line. It was fed by a variety of flammable materials such as rubber gloves and plexiglass windows in the glove boxes. Finally it found a route into the rest of the building and developed into a major conflagration. As the fire gained a hold, the firefighters who had rushed to the scene fought to control it.

They knew that when it came into contact with water, plutonium could react in an explosive and volatile manner. Known as a criticality accident, this is an uncontrolled and deadly chain reaction - effectively a nuclear explosion. Such an incident was usually marked by a blue flash of intense neutron radiation. This radiation released by a criticality accident is usually unsurvivable.

For this reason the firefighters initially used carbon dioxide extinguishers on the fire but to no avail. In desperation they then used water to dampen down the fire. Initially it worked, until there was a huge blast destroying many of the air filters and sending a plume of flame that ripped the lead cap on the building's smoke stack apart. Without the filters designed to catch radioactive particles, plutonium and other radiological isotopes began escaping into the atmosphere.

It is difficult to know how much plutonium was released. An article in Wikipedia puts the total at an estimated 1.12 pounds of plutonium to be blown downwind towards the suburbs of Denver. This may not sound like a huge quantity but it caused significant radioactive contamination in areas adjacent to the plant as well as some of Denver's suburbs. In addition to this, the plutonium particles trapped in the filters had also been released by the explosion. These filters had not been cleaned for four years in which case the amount released by the blast was significant. Nobody knows how much since all the measuring equipment was destroyed in the fire.

The U.S. Department of Energy has always denied that the 1957 fire at The Rocky Flats Plant was anything more than a conventional conflagration.(2) Others challenge this view.

One of these is the author, Kristen Iversen. In her book *Full Body Burden: Growing Up in the Nuclear Shadow of Rocky Flats* (1) she claims that the 1957 plutonium fire at the plant sparked a full criticality accident. She also asserts that the amount of radioactivity released as a result of the 1957 fire was much more extensive in both quantity and area than officially admitted. Her researches showed that not only did it blow over Denver City but 30 miles beyond. The serious nature of the 1957 fire and any information about radiation it caused was kept secret for thirteen years. In fact, it would take another catastrophic fire for the truth to finally emerge.

In the meantime, a serious radiation leakage occurred at The Rocky Flats Plant between 1964 and 1967. Less dramatic than the 1957 fire, this leakage was nevertheless important.

Milling plutonium parts for the manufacture of the bomb triggers required a considerable amount of fluid for cooling during this process. In a storage area known as Pad 903, thousands of gallons of this fluid contaminated with radioactive shavings were stored in fifty-five gallon drums. This was an open air facility with a soil base. Over the years the drums corroded allowing the radioactive fluids to drain away into the earth and local water sources. It is estimated that the total quantity of the leaked waste was about five thousand gallons. A lesser but still significant quantity dried out and mixed with ground dust eventually to be carried away by the wind.

Twelve years later, Rocky Flats experienced another fire remarkably similar to the 1957 conflagration. On 11th May 1969, plutonium particles once again spontaneously ignited in the glove boxes. They were in Building 777 (Formerly Building 71) which was the Plutonium Processing Facility. Fire suppression systems that would have cut the fire off in its early stages had not been fitted in the glove boxes. This was in spite of a recommendation after the catastrophic 1957 fire.

As the fire spread throughout the building, it had all the potential for being a worse disaster than the 1957 catastrophe. That it did not, was down to three factors. Firstly, the filters preventing radioactive particles from escaping into the atmosphere resisted the fire. This was because after the earlier fire in which the cellulose filters had all burned, their replacements had been made of non flammable fibreglass.

Secondly, a metal plate had accidentally been left in the production line of glove boxes. This had the effect of diverting the fire from Building 777 which was single storey, to the neighbouring Building 776. Fortunately, this building had two floors which acted as a shield for the roof. So, in spite of considerable fire damage, the roof of the building mercifully held. If the fire had not been accidentally diverted, the roof in Building 777 would have burned through. Since it contained an estimated total of 10,600 lb (4,500 kg) of plutonium, the amount of radioactive material released would have been on a massive scale.

A third accident fortuitously helped reduce the quantity of radioactive material released. The plant's fans were deprived of power due to a fire truck hitting a pole carrying the electrical power cables. This stopped the fans drawing the fire into the filters and towards the vulnerable roof.

Had either the roof or filters failed, the resultant radioactive contamination would have been on a much larger scale than the earlier fire. As it was, the 1969 fire caused the release of only a small amount of radioactive material into the general atmosphere.

Known as 'The Mothers Day Fire' because it occurred on the afternoon of Mothering Sunday, the 1969 conflagration proved costly both in financial and human terms. Forty-one workers at The Rocky Flats Plant were seriously irradiated and its total bill was $70 million. At the time, it was the costliest nuclear accident in U.S. history. The final clean-up took two years to complete. The repercussions from the 1969 fire would last for years and probably lead to the plant's ultimate closure in 1992.

After the Mothers Day Fire, an independent group of scientists conducted a study of the radiation levels surrounding the Rocky Flats Plant. What they were looking for was how much radiation had been released by the fire. What they actually uncovered was a thirteen year old secret as devastating as it was unexpected.

They found levels of plutonium radiation in the neighbouring areas 400 to 1,500 times higher than normal. It was only at this point that the authorities admitted what they had known all along, that the area had been contaminated with plutonium radiation for years. In fact, they said, much of it had come, not from the 1969 fire, but the 1957 conflagration. They also admitted that significant long term radiation had come from the leaking drums at Pad 903.

Unsurprisingly, the local population felt betrayed by the plant authorities and their own government. After years of being assured that the facility was absolutely safe, inhabitants of Colorado and Denver discovered they had been living with a factory leaking death on their doorstep.

From then on, opposition to the presence of the Rocky Flats Plant grew inexorably. Long term protests were mounted just beyond the plant's perimeter fence and entrances. These were organised and led by groups of activists such as The Rocky Flats Truth Force.

Despite many arrests, they continued for years with rallies of thousands demanding the cessation of Rocky Flats' nuclear manufacturing. In 1983 one such gathering attracted 17,000 people who linked hands in a human chain around the perimeter of the plant. The protests also attracted such luminaries as political activist Daniel Ellsberg and the poet Allen Ginsberg, both of whom were arrested more than once.

By 1975, Dow Chemical decided not to renew their contract to run the plant and passed the torch on to another large American corporation, Rockwell. Author Kristen Iversen feels this decision was influenced by the increasing cost of accidents at the plant and the growing protest movement.

Rockwell faced the same problems disposing radioactive waste as those experienced by the previous management. Their attempts also met with failure. They tried mixing this waste with concrete blocks in cardboard containers which were dubbed 'pondcrete'. As predicted by their own engineers, this did not work, with the concrete mixture failing to set in many cases. Once again, radiation leaked from the open air storage area into the ground.

Despite the change in management, safety concerns over the operation of Rocky Flats Plant continued to grow. Finally, on 6th June 1989, 'Operation Desert Glow' was launched. This was an FBI raid on the facility sponsored by The U.S. Department of Justice and was led by Joe Lipsky, an FBI agent. It led to the establishment of Colorado's first Special Grand Jury. Under this, a group of the State's citizens were empowered to pursue criminal proceedings against Rockwell for environmental crimes such as the illegal burning of plutonium.

During these proceedings, one hundred and ten witnesses were called with 2,000 exhibits used as evidence. Finally, Rockwell admitted to ten environmental crimes. At $18.5 million the company was given the highest fine for hazardous waste offences in U.S. history. In September 1989, Rockwell the sudden decision to withdraw from running The Rocky Flats Plant. The third company to take on this onerous and questionable task of running the plant was defence contractor E. G. & G.

Much of the work carried out by the plant's new management was in the area of cleaning up historical contamination. With the fall of the Berlin Wall and the collapse of the Soviet Union, the world had changed for Rocky Flats. The U.S. and Russia both agreed to a sharp reduction in the number of their nuclear warheads. As a result, in 1992 virtually all bomb manufacture at the plant ceased and 4,500 employees were made redundant. A further 4,000 were kept on to continue the long term clean-up operation.

In 1994 the plant was renamed The Rocky Flats Environmental Technology Site. This was intended to reflect the changed role of the site. Nuclear weaponry was no longer manufactured there. Instead, all work at Rocky Flats was dedicated to demolition, decontamination and restoration. As far as humanly possible the site was to be returned to its pre-bomb factory condition. This work would continue throughout the 1990s and 2000s.

Great concern continues to be shown by Iversen and many other activists and concerned citizens at the thoroughness or otherwise of the Rocky Flats clean-up. What was estimated to take seventy years to complete and cost $36 billion was completed in seven years by Kaiser-Hill LLC with a total bill of $7.3 billion.

The area that was cleaned up by Kaiser-Hill is now The Rocky Flats National Wildlife Refuge and is open to visitors every day of the year except for Thanksgiving, Christmas and New Years Day. It is managed by The U.S. Fish and Wildlife Service. It covers an area of 5,237 acres (21.19 km^2). An area of 1,300 acres which was the core of the Rocky Flats Plant is not part of the Refuge. It remains closed off to the public and under the management of the Department of Energy.

One of the many concerns is how many of the original plutonium particles that escaped as a result of the leaks and fires at the plant remain in the ground. The reason for this worry is the deadly long term nature of plutonium. If you get it on your skin it can be washed off, but even a minuscule particle of plutonium within your body is another matter. If a tiny fragment of plutonium is inhaled, it can lodge within the body and turn cancerous many years later.

Because of this, in 2018 the management of several school districts in Colorado banned school visits to the Refuge citing these safety concerns. Democratic politicians in Washington who represent the nearby city of Boulder City have also called for the Refuge to be closed to the public for the same reason.

The numbers of deaths and illnesses that can be directly linked to either the two fires or the leakage from the drums stored at Pad 903 are hard to pin down.

Dr. John Cobb at the University of Colorado reported that lung and liver tissue taken during autopsies from the bodies of 450 people who lived near Rocky Flats all contained plutonium.

Another local medical man who was convinced the presence of the Rocky Flats Plant was not conducive to the public health was Dr Carl Johnson, the Jefferson County Health Director at the time. In 1976 he opposed housing developments close to the Plant because of the high levels of harmful radiation he found there. His findings showed that soil on land adjacent to the Rocky Flats Plant had 44 times more plutonium than the government admitted.

In 1977 he made further alarming discoveries. Firstly that there were leukaemia and cancer spikes in the local population. Secondly that the number of brain tumours suffered by workers at the Rocky Flats Plant was eight times higher than it should be. In 1981 he was fired for making waves but later won a 'whistleblower' lawsuit against his employers.

Much of what Johnson said at the time was subsequently proved to be accurate. Sadly he would not live to see the Rocky Flats Plant closed since he died in 1988.

Although the Secretary of the Interior has now ruled that the Rocky Flats National Wildlife Refuge is safe enough for visits by children on school field trips, concern and controversy continue to cloud its future.

Local people who know the full history of Rocky Flats, complain that new residents moving into urban developments in the area are wilfully ignorant of the perceived danger from residual radiation. They feel that these 'newbies' either don't know or *don't want to know* about these risks.

In a 2018 article in *Westword*, a Denver newspaper and online news journal, local librarian Ron Baxendale II summed local feeling up very succinctly in an Op Ed article entitled *"The Dangers of Rocky Flats Are Forgotten but Not Gone."* Addressing one of the new Colorado residents and 'naysayers', he had this to say about his own family's health problems: *"My paternal grandmother died of brain cancer. That my aunt died of rare liver cancer and my fifty-year-old cousin of uterine cancer. That my mom had symptoms of MS before contracting colon cancer and then dying of peritoneal cancer. That my dad suffers from prostate cancer, my sister from MS, and my brother from a string of undiagnosed illnesses. And that I've had three surgeries for thyroid cancer."*

Today, the stunningly beautiful landscape around the former Rocky Flats Plant gives no hint of its past. It has a deceptively pristine appearance. Whether or not the fears regarding long term radiation are borne out will only become apparent in years to come. Time will tell.

Sources

(1) Kristen Iversen was brought up close to the Rocky Flats Plant in Colorado and actually worked there for a while. *Full Body Burden: Growing Up in the Nuclear Shadow of Rocky Flats* is part memoir and part journalistic investigation into the history of The Rocky Flats Plant including the two big fires and the radiation leak at Pad 903. It is available from Amazon in Kindle, paperback and hardback editions.
A September 11th Catastrophe You've Probably Never Heard About.
Andrew Cohen, *Atlantic Monthly Magazine* September 10th, 2012

(2) The 1957 Fire at Rocky Flats *"resulted in no spread of radioactive contamination of any consequence"* - An Atomic Energy Commission spokesman quoted by *The Denver Post* 12th September 1957

Rocky Flats Nuclear Weapons Plant prior to clean up.
Photograph: US Department of Energy

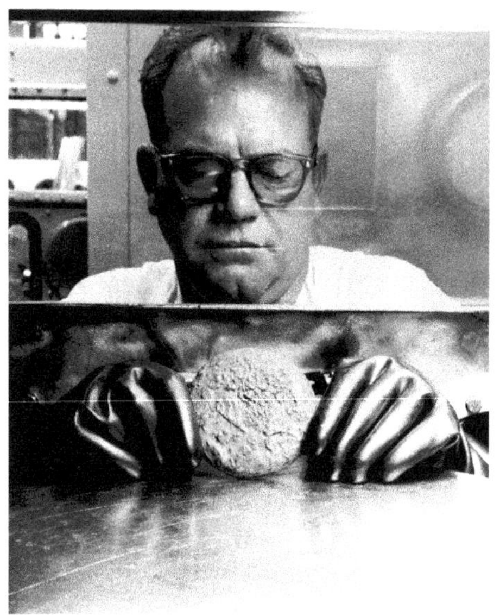

Employee working on a plutonium core in a glovebox at The Rocky Flats Plant.

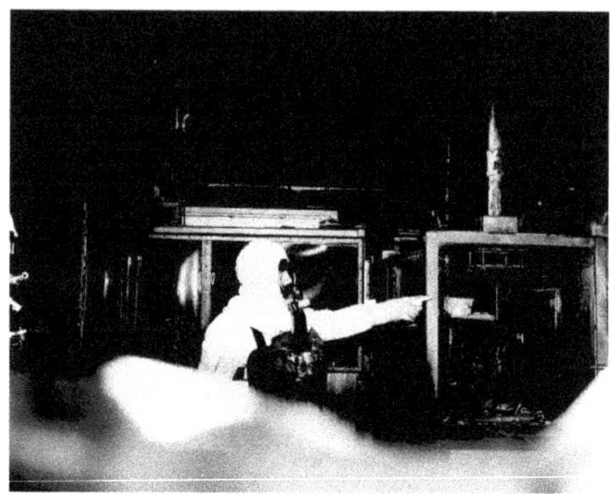

The glove boxes where the 1957 fire started at The Rocky Flats Plant.

Corroded drum containing nuclear waste at Pad 903, The Rocky Flats Plant.

Damage from the 1957 fire at The Rocky Flats Plant.

Chapter 6
A Question of Criticality

Since the dawn of the nuclear age in the 1940s, there have been about sixty accidental chain reactions known as criticality accidents. Although small in number when set against all the nuclear accidents and events that have occurred, they are a sobering reminder of the power of the atom.

Criticality accidents often have several characteristics in common; they are usually accompanied by an intense electric blue flash resulting from the creation of electromagnetic radiation during the accident. Such accidents produce high levels of radiation that are usually fatal and there is often a strong ozone smell and a metallic taste in the mouth. This smell and taste was reported by survivors of Chernobyl and the Vinča nuclear reactor accidents.

Here, in chronological order are some of the most notable criticality accidents:

Los Alamos
1944 - 1946

The first six such incidents happened at the birthplace of the Atomic bomb, Los Alamos National Laboratory in New Mexico. They all happened during experiments linked to the development of nuclear weapons.

In the 1940s its scientists constructed a small nuclear reactor for producing intense bursts of radiation. Presumably because the machine was unshielded they named it *Lady Godiva* in honour of history's most famous naked lady. Within it was a piece of uranium 235 measuring a foot in diameter into which a rod of another fissile material was rapidly inserted and extracted. This briefly created a critical mass sparking a chain reaction which released a stream of neutrons and gamma rays. These would then irradiate test samples.

One of the leading scientists working in this field was Austrian born Otto Robert Frisch. In 1944 during one of these early fission experiments Frisch leaned a little too close to *Lady Godiva*. Some of the neutrons emanating from the uranium in *Godiva* bounced back from his body creating the critical mass to spark an accidental chain reaction. Fortunately, Frisch noticed that the red warning lights which normally flickered when neutrons were emitted were shining constantly. Realising this signalled a criticality accident, he quickly leant away from the machine and removed some of the uranium. This stopped the chain reaction. Had Frisch been a bit slower off the mark he would have been fatally irradiated.

Two more criticality accidents occurred within *Lady Godiva* in 1954 and 1957. The second one damaged the machine beyond repair. Fortunately nobody was killed or injured in either of these events. A number of criticality accidents also occurred in other laboratories at Los Alamos

On 4th June 1945 a Los Alamos scientist called John Bistline was conducting an experiment with enriched uranium and water when something went wrong with near fatal consequences. A chain reaction was sparked when the two elements accidentally came into contact with one another. Three people were injured by the radiation released during this accident but nobody died.

Harry Daghlian was another scientist working in this risky field at Los Alamos. On 21st August 1945 he was attempting to build a shield of tungsten bricks around a ball of plutonium. In doing this he was hoping to reflect neutrons back at the plutonium thereby creating a critical mass using less fissile material. In doing so, he dropped one of the tungsten bricks on the plutonium globe in the centre of the assembly (*see photograph page 54*). This kick started an uncontrollable chain reaction and criticality accident.

Whilst trying to halt the reaction by removing the tungsten bricks Daghlian received a fatal dose of radiation. Daghlian must have known this action would sign his death warrant and selflessly did this to protect his colleagues. He died 25 days later from radiation poisoning. This earned him the sad distinction of being the first fatality of a criticality accident. In fact he was probably the first fatality of the nuclear age.

In May 1946, a close colleague of Daghlian at Los Alamos, Canadian scientist, Louis Slotin was experimenting with the creation of an early stage in fission reaction for nuclear weapons. In his case two hollow half spheres or cups of radioactive beryllium were being kept apart from the same globe of plutonium that Daghlian used. One was just above and the other just below the plutonium. This whole construct was set up on a bench in the middle of a laboratory. The beryllium and plutonium had to be kept separate to prevent a chain reaction occurring suddenly by accident.

The screwdriver that Slotin was using for this purpose (*see photograph of re-enactment on page 55*) eventually slipped and the two beryllium hemispheres closed round the plutonium creating a critical mass. This caused an extreme chain reaction releasing an intense burst of radiation. Slotin caught the brunt of this and died of radiation poisoning on 30th May 1946, nine days after the accident.

The seven other scientists observing the experiment in the room at the time reported seeing the characteristic blue glow that occurs in such accidental chain reactions. They all received doses of radiation of varying degrees of severity and none died immediately. However, at least one was left with long term health issues related to the accident and three others died early as a result of the radiation they received. Like Daghlian, Slotin rapidly dismantled the device separating the beryllium hemispheres from the plutonium. This stopped the chain reaction saving the lives of the seven observers.

Following the Slotin criticality accident, all other hands-on experiments were banned. Future tests were carried out on a remote control basis with operatives and scientists shielded in a separate room.

A re-creation of the 'Demon Core' which Harry Daghlian conducted his experiment in August 21st 1945 that led to the fatal criticality accident.
Photograph: Los Alamos National Laboratory/U.S. Government

Footnote
The Demon Core

Measuring only three and a half inches in diameter, about the size of a grapefruit, the drab grey ball of plutonium used in the Los Alamos experiments did not look much. Nevertheless, as the Daghlian and Slotin accidents showed, this core could easily become lethal even in the hands of the most experienced scientists. In both these tragic cases, simple accidents sealed the fate of both men. After their deaths the plutonium core earned the sinister nickname 'Demon Core' amongst the scientists at Los Alamos. Its lethal potential also gave experiments with plutonium cores the name '*Tickling the Dragon's tail*'.

'Tickling the Dragon's Tail'. Recreation of Louis Slotin's last fatal experiment using a screwdriver that led to a criticality accident.
Photograph: Los Angeles National Laboratory/U.S.Government

Sources

The Demon Core and the Strange Death of Louis Slotin By Alex Wellerstein
New Yorker May 21st 2016
Review of Criticality Accidents 2000 Los Alamos National Laboratory

Idaho National Laboratory
Idaho Falls, Idaho, US
October 1956

During the early years of the Cold War, the U.S. Government was looking to develop nuclear powered jet aircraft. The advantage of such aircraft was that the nuclear fuel powering their reactors only needed replacing after years. On the other hand, conventionally powered aircraft needed to refuel at regular intervals of hours or days. This usually involved risky in-flight operations. So, unlike conventionally powered bombers nuclear powered jets could stay airborne for long periods of time stretching from weeks to months.

With this in mind, a series of experiments were initiated at the Idaho National Laboratory, a world leader in such advanced technology. In 1956 a nuclear reactor was used to power a General Electric J47 aircraft engine on a test bed at the Laboratory. These tests were known as Heat Transfer Reactor Experiments or HTRE with the number of each experiment tacked on the end i.e. HTRE - 1.

On 31st October 1956, during the HTRE - 3 test a serious fault developed in the reactor controls. This caused the control rods in the reactor to be drawn out too far triggering an uncontrolled chain reaction. The reactor suffered a partial meltdown before matters were brought under control. Fortunately, this criticality accident caused no injuries or fatalities.

Experimentation into developing nuclear powered aircraft would continue for another fifteen years. Despite the expenditure of $1 billion, a flying nuclear powered aircraft still had not been produced. As a result, President Kennedy cancelled the project on 26th March 1961.

Oak Ridge Uranium Plant
Oak Ridge, Anderson & Roane Counties
Tennessee. U.S.
16th June 1958

The town of Oak Ridge in the State of Tennessee was created in 1942 to house workers for the Oak Ridge Nuclear Complex established there. That was a facility to manufacture materials for the *Manhattan* A-bomb project. It was selected by the federal U.S. Government for a number of reasons including the secrecy afforded by its relatively secluded location and the low purchase cost of the local land. This was an important factor since the project needed 60,000 acres of land. The whole area was declared a military district by Presidential Decree in 1943.

Because of these far reaching requirements, Prentice Cooper, the Governor of Tennessee at the time was strongly opposed to the project. It did not help that he was initially informed of it by a junior military officer. After a more tactful approach by senior members of the armed forces he was won round.

Once established, the nuclear facility grew rapidly with the K-25 Uranium Processing Facility covering 44 acres in 1945. With the influx of plant workers the town of Oak Ridge grew from a population of 3,750 at its inception in 1942 to approximately 75,000 at the end of the war.

For the first twenty-six years of its existence, the plant processed uranium safely and without incident. Then in 1958 came a wake up call.

On 16th June of that year, during a test for leaks at the Y-12 Uranium Processing Plant at Oak Ridge, a quantity of fissile material, probably uranium 235 accidentally collected in a 55 gallon drum. The amount must have been sufficient to form a critical mass since it sparked a chain reaction. This criticality accident lasted for twenty minutes before being curbed.

During this time eight workers received significant doses of radiation with five of them being hospitalised for forty-four days. They all recovered and returned to work. There were no fatalities. This was the first time a criticality accident was linked to uranium processing. By any standards, it was a close call which could have been so much worse.

After The Second World War, the Oak Ridge Complex was turned over to civilian control with many of its buildings being demolished over the next forty to fifty years. Two survivors are S-12, the plant originally used for electromagnetic separation of uranium. It now processes and stores materials for nuclear weapons. X-10, the building that housed an experimental graphite reactor is now The Oak Ridge National Laboratory. It was here in 2018 that '*Summit*' the world's fastest super computer was introduced to the public. It is a joint venture by the Laboratory and IBM.

Vinča Nuclear Institute
Yugoslavia
October 1958

On 15th October 1958, six young research students were allowed in to work on one of two reactors at the Vinča Nuclear Institute near Belgrade in communist Yugoslavia. Permission to do research on such a security sensitive facility was a big privilege in the communist state. In view of this, they must have had a very high trust rating with the authorities. It seems they were conducting some experiments for a thesis by one of the students.

Apparently, these experiments involved 3,995 kg of uranium coated in aluminium foil. The uranium was submerged in the heavy water within one of the Institute's two reactors. This was done so that the heavy water could act as a brake on any uncontrolled chain reaction.

Somewhere along the line a criticality accident happened in the heavy water reactor known as RB. One of the researchers was alerted to this after ten minutes by the characteristic smell of ozone from the chain reaction. All six students received high doses of radiation before the chain reaction was brought under control.

Suffering from radiation sickness, they were all hospitalised in Belgrade where one of them died. The five survivors were then transferred to the Marie Curie Institute in France that had specialist knowledge of treating patients suffering from the effects of radiation.

Once there, the institute's oncologist Georges Mahé performed the first successful bone marrow transplants in the world on them. Four of the marrow recipients survived and recovered to return to their research work in Belgrade. A few years later, one of the survivors, Rosanda Dangubic, gave birth to a healthy baby girl. Considering the amount of radiation she absorbed in the accident, it is a miracle she was not rendered infertile.

Sources

Vinca reactor accident, 1958. Robert Johnston Archive 2005

A Review of Criticality Accidents, 2000 Revision, Los Alamos National Laboratory (Los Alamos, NM)

Cecil Kelley's Criticality Accident Los Alamos 30th December 1958

By 1958 Cecil Kelley had notched up eleven and a half years experience as a chemical operator in the nuclear industry over half which had been at the Los Alamos complex. What happened to him on 30th December of that year shows that even the most experienced personnel can fall foul of unexpected accidents. When this happens in a nuclear context, it often leads to tragedy.

On that particular day Kelley was operating a 1000 litre stainless steel mixing tank. It was just one of many jobs he did at Los Alamos. The main purpose of this tank was to dissolve nuclear waste from experiments so that valuable material such as plutonium could be recovered and reused. On this occasion the stainless steel tank contained plutonium-239. As part of this recycling process, the plutonium was dissolved in nitric acid.

At some stage, what was officially called 'two improper transfers' took place. This was the incorrect addition of a further 3 kilograms of plutonium rich liquid waste into the mixing tank taking the total quantity of plutonium in the tank to its critical mass where a chain reaction would take place. To this day, nobody knows who added that deadly extra quantity of plutonium to what was already in the tank. The only reason a criticality accident had not been triggered was that the rich and lean plutonium waste solutions were separated from one another by weight. Being heavier, the lean solution gravitated to the bottom of the tank whilst the lighter rich solution floated at the surface.

When Kelley came to operate the stirrer in the tank he was totally unaware of the radioactive witches brew that lay in wait for him. For all he knew, the tank contained a uniformly lean mixture of dissolved plutonium. If this had been the case, the quantity of plutonium would have measured less than 0.1 grams per litre which was well below the danger level where a critical mass would cause an explosion. In fact the concentration of plutonium was 200 times higher than that.

When Kelley turned on the stirrer in the tank it created a vortex bringing the 'lean' solution of plutonium waste at the bottom of the tank to mix with the much richer solution at the surface. This created a critical mass which triggered a criticality accident.

Instantly, a chain reaction started with a blue flash seen by two other operatives. Kelley, who had been observing the mixing process through an observation window fell off the ladder on which he was standing. It is probable that the burst of energy from the chain reaction was responsible for this.

Temporarily disoriented from this fall, Kelley switched the mixers on and off in quick succession before running out of the building. His colleagues found him lying on the snow in convulsions and crying "I'm burning up! I'm burning up!"

The chain reaction had also released a massive level of radioactivity that fatally irradiated the unfortunate Kelley. He had been hit by more than seven times the human lethal dose of radiation. The medics fought hard to save his life including giving him numerous blood transfusions. This did not work and he died thirty five hours after the accident.

A public explanation how the extra plutonium waste came to be in the mixer tank which caused the accident was never given. Inevitably Kelley was blamed for accidentally adding too much plutonium to the mix. It seems difficult to believe that such an experienced operative would knowingly take such a risky and careless course of action.

A detailed description of this accident in *A Review of Criticality Accidents 2000* published by The Los Alamos National Laboratory states: *A reconstruction of significant events indicates that unexpected plutonium rich solids, which should have been handled separately, were washed from two vessels into a single large vessel that contained dilute aqueous and organic solutions.*

This rather bland official description of the cause of the accident hides its full tragic impact. As in most of the cases covered in this book, such incidents carry with them a backstory of human suffering.

With Cecil Kelley this involved his wife Doris and their two children aged eight years and eighteen months. Initially, Mrs Kelley was not informed of her husband's irradiation accident until after his death. Denying her the opportunity to see her husband one last time sounds very heartless. It should be borne in mind the level of radioactivity in his body probably made it dangerous for her to be anywhere near him. The authorities at Los Alamos may also have considered Kelley's final appearance before his death to have been too distressing for his widow to witness.

Doris Kelley was assured by the Los Alamos Laboratory management that she would be adequately compensated for her husband's tragic death.

What this amounted to was a low paid job for life with the Laboratory. Years later she actually received the compensation she should have been paid in the first place, but not in the way she or her late husband's employers envisaged.

During the post mortem on Cecil Kelley's body, pathologists removed three kilograms of his tissue. This was used for research into the effect of radiation on the human body. This would be the first of many unauthorised tissue removals conducted by the pathologists at Los Alamos

In 1998, Doris Kelley and her daughter Katie Kelley-Mareau and others filed a class action against the Los Alamos Laboratory and the pathologist who performed the post mortem on Kelley's body. It alleged misconduct because permission had not been sought from the next of kin to remove organs from the deceased's body. In 2002 the plaintiffs were awarded $9.5 million and a further $800,000 in 2007. The defendants did not admit to any wrongdoing.

Sources

Andrews, L. Nelkin, D. (1998). 'Whose body is it anyway? Disputes over body tissue in a biotechnology age.' Lancet 1998

Review of Criticality Accidents 2000 Los Alamos National Laboratory

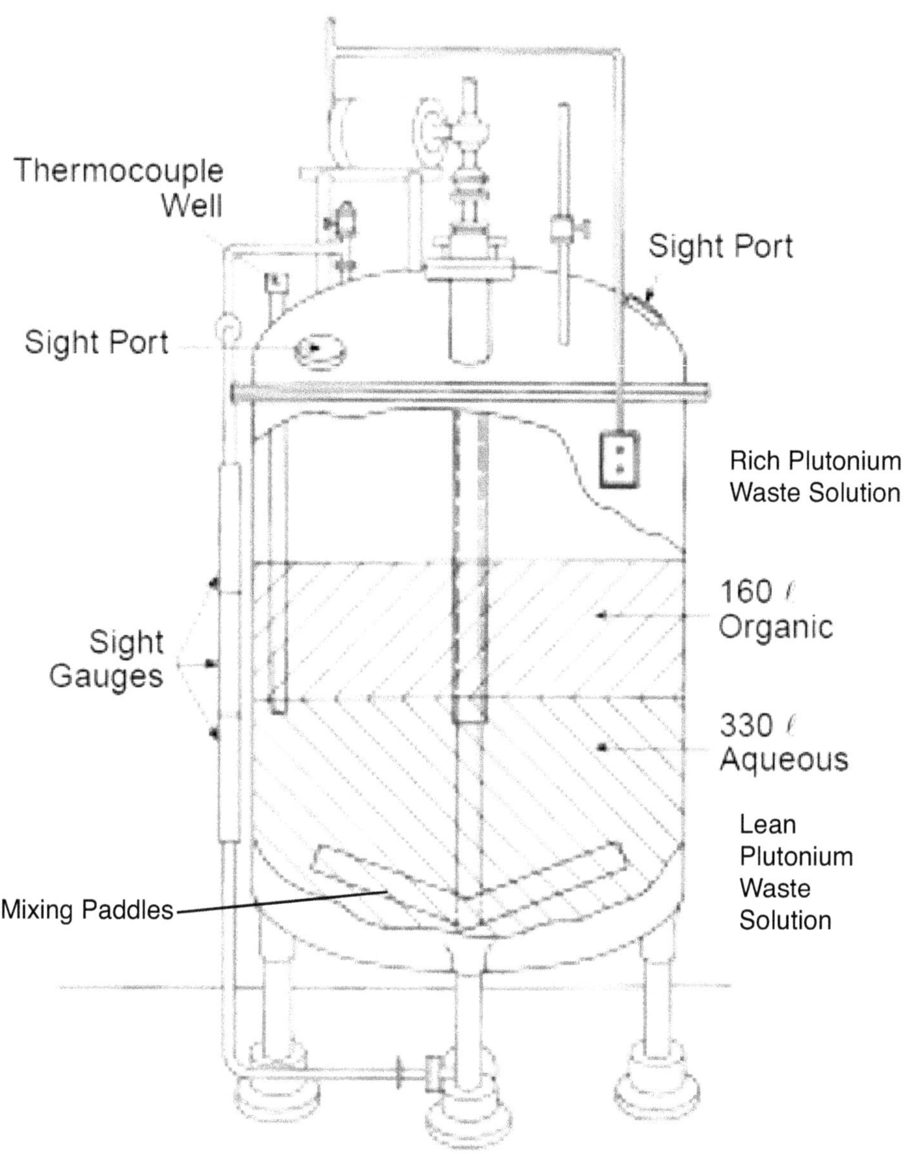

Diagram of the 1000 litre mixing vessel in which the criticality accident that irradiated and killed Cecil Kelley occurred on 30th December 1958. The rich and lean mixtures are shown in the tank.

Image: Los Alamos Nat Laboratory/US Department of Energy

The Wood River Tragedy
Wood River Junction
Rhode Island, United States
24th July 1964

The United Nuclear Corporation (UNC) plant near Wood River Junction in rural Rhode Island was designed to reprocess nuclear waste. This arrived at the plant primarily in the form of scrap such as spent nuclear fuel rods containing highly enriched uranium. The scrap would be dissolved in tanks and vats of acid allowing the valuable but highly dangerous uranium to be filtered off.

Opened in the early spring of 1964, Wood River was considered to be the technological flagship of UNC. The company itself was pretty new, having been formed out of three other major corporations in 1961. It was in the summer of '64 that a tragic accident would mar the new plant's safety record. It proved to be remarkably similar to the one that befell Cecil Kelley.

Robert Peabody was a 37 year old local man who worked as a production technician at the plant. Having been employed in the U.S. nuclear industry for fourteen years, he had considerable experience. On Friday 24th July 1964, he was working the night shift at the plant. This allowed him to do his other 'day job' at an auto workshop. Whilst conditions and pay were good at the UNC plant, with nine children, Robert needed all the money he could earn to keep his family afloat.

During the shift, Peabody worked on a tank that contained uranium 235 dissolved in a solution of sodium carbonate. Uranium is pretty dangerous stuff especially when enough of it is combined to 'go critical' and cause a chain reaction. However, the quantity dissolved in this tank was safely below the critical mass.

At some stage during the shift, Peabody added what he thought was trichloroethane (basically dry cleaning fluid) from one of a number of 11 litre (625 pint) 'safe geometry' bottles. Measuring five inches in diameter and four feet long, these containers were specifically designed to hold uranium and other radioactive solutions in a safe state. The 'safe geometry' shape of the bottle ensured that the uranium at the top did not coalesce with that at the bottom causing it to go critical.

The bottles containing chemicals such as trichloroethane were identical and could only be identified by their labels. These were secured just by elastic bands and not any form of adhesive. As a result these labels tended to come loose and drop off.

Unfortunately, this was just what happened with the bottle that Robert Peabody selected. Thinking he had one of the bottles that only contained trichloroethane, he emptied its contents into the mixing tank. In fact it contained a rich solution of uranium waste and not just the chemical he thought. Once in the mixer tank the additional uranium took the whole quantity above the safety level to a critical mass. This immediately sparked an uncontrolled chain reaction. The explosion that followed spewed out about ten litres of highly radioactive waste from the tank accompanied by a flash of blue light.

Peabody, like the victims of so many other criticality accidents, received a massive and fatal dose of radiation. It was later estimated that he had been exposed to 10,000 rad of radiation. This was way above the lethal amount for a human being. He was rushed to the local hospital at the nearby town of Westerly.

With no facilities to deal with radiation, the ambulance was sent to the main hospital in Providence, Rhode Island's capital. Two days after the accident, most of which were in acute pain and agony, Robert Peabody slipped into a coma and died on the Sunday night.

The United Nuclear Corporation was charged by the Atomic Energy Commission with 14 violations of nuclear safety regulations, eight of which related to the accident that killed Peabody. According to an article by Dennis Powell in *Yankee Magazine (Incident at Wood River Junction October 1994),* these were never paid. The same article stated that Peabody's widow Anna received $22,000 settlement as a result of a lawsuit. Whilst this was a significant sum of money in 1964, it was hardly adequate compensation for the loss of a beloved husband or enough to bring up nine children.

The Wood River Junction Plant continued operating until its closure in 1980. During that time much of the chemical and radionuclide waste from the facility was discharged from the plant into the surrounding environment including the nearby Pawcatuck River. After the closure, United Nuclear and the federal government launched a multi million dollar clean-up of the 1,114 acre site. Much of the old site is now a nature reserve.

In the following years, United Nuclear Corporation either closed or divested itself of its remaining nuclear facilities. This included their laboratory at Pawling in New York State which closed after a plutonium explosion occurred in a glove box. Work at this facility was shrouded in secrecy so whether the accident was caused by too much plutonium in the glove box leading to an uncontrolled chain reaction is not known. In the event, one lab technician suffered non fatal injuries. A 'low level of radiation' contaminated the lab building. The clean up after this accident cost $3 million and lasted two years.

Sources

Incident at Wood River Junction Yankee Magazine October 1994
Tragic Death Gives Way to Environmental Rebirth Article from ecoRI.org website (Rhode Island Ecological group) January 6th, 2016

RA - 2 Reactor Accident Centro Atomico Constituyentes Buenos Aires Argentina 23rd September 1983

Argentina's involvement in nuclear power goes back further than any other South American country. In 1957, the government opened the continent's first nuclear research reactor. In addition to this, The Balseiro Institute in Bariloche is considered to be the leader in nuclear research in Latin America, if not the world.

The military dictatorship in Argentina during the 1980s had an active nuclear weapons programme. To this end, the civilian side of nuclear research and development was absorbed into the military programme. During this period, two missiles were developed, the Alacran (Scorpion) and Condor 2.

The RA-2 experimental reactor near the capital Buenos Aires was also part of this programme. On 23rd September 1983 a technician with fourteen years experience was changing the configuration of the fuel rods in the reactor. The chamber of the reactor was filled with de-mineralised water at the time. According to procedures this water should have been drained during this procedure.

The operator was half way through placing the second of two control elements within the fuel configuration of the reactor when an accidental chain reaction was sparked. This immediately released an intense burst of radiation which gave the operative a fatal dose.
He died after two days.

Eight other technicians not immediately inside the building housing the reactor received lesser doses of radiation from which they survived. At the time of writing, I have not been able to ascertain whether the failure to drain the de-mineralised water modulator from the reactor caused the accidental chain reaction. The RA-2 Research reactor was closed down in September 1983, presumably as a result of this tragic accident. The return to civilian rule in Argentina in the same year marked the end of the country's ambitions of becoming a military nuclear power and the nascent nuclear weapons programme was abandoned. However, the country continues to have an active nuclear power programme for peaceful purposes.

Russian Federal Nuclear Centre Sarov. Russian Federation 17th June 1997

Sarov has long been one of Russia's 'closed cities'. Since 1946 it has been the centre of that country's nuclear research programme. For a long time it was known only as Arzamas-16 and was removed from all maps. It was while he was working at Russian Federal Nuclear Centre in the city in 1997 that scientist Alexander Zakharov was involved in a fatal criticality accident.

It seems that he was conducting an experiment that was very similar to the ones performed by Daghlian and Slotin at Los Alamos. In the Russian's case the materials he was using were a core of uranium, copper shielding and other fissile materials. Like the Los Alamos experiments, Zakharov's also led to an accidental chain reaction. According to the *Review of Criticality Accidents* by the Los Alamos Laboratory this accident was partly caused by the researcher getting the calculations for his experimental machine assembly wrong.

At 10:40 in the morning of 17th June 1997 the uranium and fissile materials in the assembly accidentally combined to form a critical mass leading to a series of uncontrollable chain reactions. Zakharov was alerted to this by a sudden blue flash characteristic of criticality accidents. He immediately left the laboratory, but it was too late. He had already received a huge dose of radiation which was unsurvivable.

He died three days later of radiation poisoning in a Moscow hospital. The chain reactions in his experimental assembly were not brought under control until a quarter to one on the morning of 24th June. Following this accident, any further such experiments were forbidden pending safety upgrades.

Chapter 7
The Windscale Fire, Cumberland (Cumbria) England, 10th October 1957

On October 10th 1957 the Tuohy family in the little Cumberland village of Beckermet had a mini crisis on their hands. Mrs Tuohy and all three of her children were laid low with a nasty dose of the 'flu. As the only fit member of the family, husband Tom was left to cope as best he could. Whilst attending to his sick family, the phone rang. It was his boss the General Manager at the Windscale nuclear plant close to the village

"You must come at once Tom," his boss said tersely, "'Pile Number One is on fire."

Telling his wife and children to stay indoors and keep all the doors and windows closed, Tom went immediately to Windscale where he was Deputy General Manager.

The Windscale Nuclear Processing facility had been built in great haste in the early 1950s to produce weapons grade plutonium for Britain's H-bomb. This had been necessary because the close co-operation between Great Britain and America on developing early nuclear weapons during The Second World War had cooled markedly in the post war years.

A watershed event in this deteriorating relationship had been the Atomic Energy Act (McMahon Act) passed by the U.S. Congress in 1946 which effectively cut off all technical co-operation relating to nuclear research with America's allies.

From the British viewpoint this looked as if America was retreating into its pre-war isolationist carapace. Indeed, there was a genuine fear that in a future conflict the United Kingdom might face hostile forces such as the Soviet Union on its own. Hence the speed at which the British embarked on developing their own nuclear weapons.

To produce the plutonium at Windscale, two reactors, also known as piles, were constructed side by side. At the core of these reactors were two large blocks of graphite. This material was used because of its properties in moderating or controlling the release of neutrons during a chain reaction.

Twelve inch long rods of uranium 236 encased in aluminium cartridges would be pushed through channels drilled into these graphite blocks. The uranium would then fuel the chain reaction used to create plutonium. At the end of these channels, the cartridges containing the spent uranium fuel dropped into a channel of water to cool them down. Once this had happened they would be collected for the plutonium isotopes to be separated from the rest of the uranium.

This whole reaction process created a high level of heat that could cause a catastrophic explosion if it was not carefully controlled. It was for this reason that the uranium was enclosed in aluminium tubes since exposure to the atmosphere causes it to heat up rapidly and uncontrollably. Giant fans were also installed at the entry point of the channels running through the graphite block to control the temperature of the reactors. The surface of the aluminium canisters were also finned to allow the air from the fans to pass over them thus further controlling the temperature of the uranium.

There were also large chimneys at the channel exits where the canisters dropped into the water cooling channels. These were designed to carry away the hot air created by the reaction process. In theory, this hot air should contain no radiation.

Fortunately, Terence Price, one of the physicists working on the construction of the reactor chimneys was far sighted enough to ask two crucial questions: What if one of the canisters missed the cooling channel and broke open? Was it not possible that radioactive elements of the uranium and plutonium could then be sucked up the chimney and into the wider atmosphere? Initially, Price's concerns were dismissed as being too far fetched and difficult to deal with. Fortunately, the leader of the project, Sir John Cockroft shared Price's concerns. Ignoring the naysayers, he insisted that scrubbers or filters be fitted to the chimneys to help prevent the accidental escape of any radioactivity into the atmosphere. At the time these were dubbed 'Cockroft's Follies' because of their cost. In the event, it was Cockroft and Price who would have the last laugh.

A thick concrete wall was also constructed around the reactor to shield the surrounding environment from any possible accidental escape of radiation.

In fact, the breaking open of some of the uranium canisters as envisaged by Price and Cockroft became a relatively common occurrence. This happened not only on the floor of the cooling chamber when they missed the water channel but also inside the graphite channels. This would occur if too much pressure was accidentally applied when forcing them through the reactor.

Initially, this is what the team of workers operating the reactor thought had happened in Pile 1 when the fire broke out. Three days before, they had noticed that the Pile 1 reactor was heating up abnormally. If this was not addressed, it could cause the reactor to explode with catastrophic results.

To rectify the problem, the team triggered a Wigner Release. Put simply this is a process whereby the graphite is heated up to 250 degrees centigrade causing it to become plastic and malleable. This meant that its temperature could be brought into line with the uranium and the whole reactor would heat up uniformly. Without the sharp difference in temperatures between the graphite and uranium the danger of one or more of the canisters breaking open or even catching fire could be prevented. As the Wigner Release ended, temperatures within the reactor would then fall to normal levels.

On this occasion the Wigner Release seemed to work when temperatures across the whole reactor core eventually began to fall. It soon became apparent however, that in one channel, number 2053, temperatures were still rising with the danger of an uncontrolled chain reaction. A second Wigner Release was ordered which apparently did the trick with temperatures throughout the whole reactor rising at a uniform and controlled rate.

Worryingly, by the early morning of October 10th the temperatures in the core of Pile 1 had not dropped as was usually the case with a Wigner Release. Instead they ratcheted upwards eventually reaching 400 degrees centigrade. Assuming a canister had simply broken open in Channel 2053, the team speeded up the fans to increase the airflow and cool things down.

What they did not know was that one of the aluminium canisters of uranium had not only broken open it had also caught fire. Increasing the airflow simply fanned the flames, worsening the whole situation. As the temperature of the core continued to increase, the team realised there was a fire in one or more of the graphite channels. They tried to confirm this with a scanner but it jammed at the crucial moment.

Tom Hughes who, as Deputy Reactor Manager, was the most senior man on site, realised there was nothing for it but to make a visual examination of the channels in the core. So he and another operator went to the charge face of the reactor and looked at the fuel channels through an inspection portal. What they saw to their horror were in his words "four channels of fuel glowing red cherry hot."

On arrival at the stricken reactor, one of Tuohy's first actions speaks volumes about his bravery and dedication. He removed his radiation recording badge so that he could not be signed off for exceeding the permitted radiation dose. He then climbed up the eighty foot pile and looked down through one of the inspection portals. What he saw was a major conflagration raging inside the reactor that must have been alight for many hours.

Over the next twenty four hours Tuohy, Hughes and their team tried everything they could to dampen the fire but without success. Increasing the airflow from the fans merely fed the flames. Next, they tried to create a firebreak by forcing some of the burning fuel cartridges out into the cooling pond. They refused to budge and some of the scaffolding rods the team were using to push the canisters melted in the extreme heat.

While all this was going on, Tuohy made repeated trips up the pile to observe what was happening to the fire. He must have known that even clad in protective clothing there was a danger this would expose his body to dangerous levels of radiation.

By the following morning, the fire was at its height with temperatures reaching 1,300 degrees centigrade in some parts of the core. In one desperate measure the team lowered 25 tons of carbon dioxide into the blazing core. When this failed to have any effect, Tom Tuohy decided on using water as a last resort.

This was a high risk strategy since the mixing of water with gas and air could have caused a massive explosion blowing the whole pile apart. They were however, out of options. If the fire was not tamed soon, it could well cause the concrete shield around the reactor to fracture and crumble in the extreme heat. The consequences of the subsequent radiation leak into the surrounding countryside did not bear thinking about.

As the water was poured into the blazing pile only Tuohy and the Chief Fire Officer remained in the reactor chamber. Mercifully, the feared explosion did not occur and finally, after a further five hours, the fire died.

It had been *a damn close run thing* as the Duke of Wellington once said of an earlier crucial battle. As it was, a significant amount of radiation was released through the reactor chimney in spite of the filters. Had these not been in place, the radioactive contamination would have been much worse.

There was a high concentration of iodine 131 in this radiation which is thought to have led to an additional 240 local cases of thyroid cancer although *at the time*, no fatalities were linked to the accident. Milk produced in a 500 square kilometre area around Windscale was also considered to be dangerously contaminated and had to be disposed of. This was done by diluting it by a thousand and then pouring it into the Irish Sea. Fears that this would adversely affect the marine life have not been borne out.

The Windscale reactors containing a significant amount of radioactive material have remained sealed since the accident. Their final decommissioning is not planned until 2037.

At Level 5 on the International Nuclear Event Scale, the Windscale fire remains Britain's worst nuclear accident. It is worth pointing out that thanks to the bravery and dedication of Tom Tuohy and his team, it could have been a great deal worse as other disasters in this book demonstrate.

In view of the role that Tom Tuohy and others played in this drama one would have thought their heroism would have been officially recognised. Shamefully, they never received any award. It was almost as if the government of the day was desperate to cover up this 'embarrassing episode'. In fact, at one stage there were official efforts to blame the accident on the workforce much to Tuohy's disgust.

It is worth noting that Sir William Penney who conducted the official enquiry into the Windscale Fire sixteen days after it was extinguished commended those involved. He stated that the measures they took were '*prompt and efficient and displayed considerable devotion to duty on the part of all concerned.*'

It has subsequently been discovered that the radiation that escaped during the Windscale Fire also contained some highly radioactive polonium 210 isotopes. The radioactive trace spread as far as Norway. Although never officially linked to radioactivity from the Windscale Fire, the subsequate death toll from cancer is thought to be between 100 and 240 fatalities.

Tom Tuohy went on to pursue a successful career in the nuclear industry. He did receive a CBE in 1969 but this was not related to the Windscale Fire. In spite of his exposure to potentially dangerous levels of radiation during the fire he never suffered any ill effects, dying at the age of 90 in 2008. Since the accident, no other air cooled reactors have been built in the U.K.

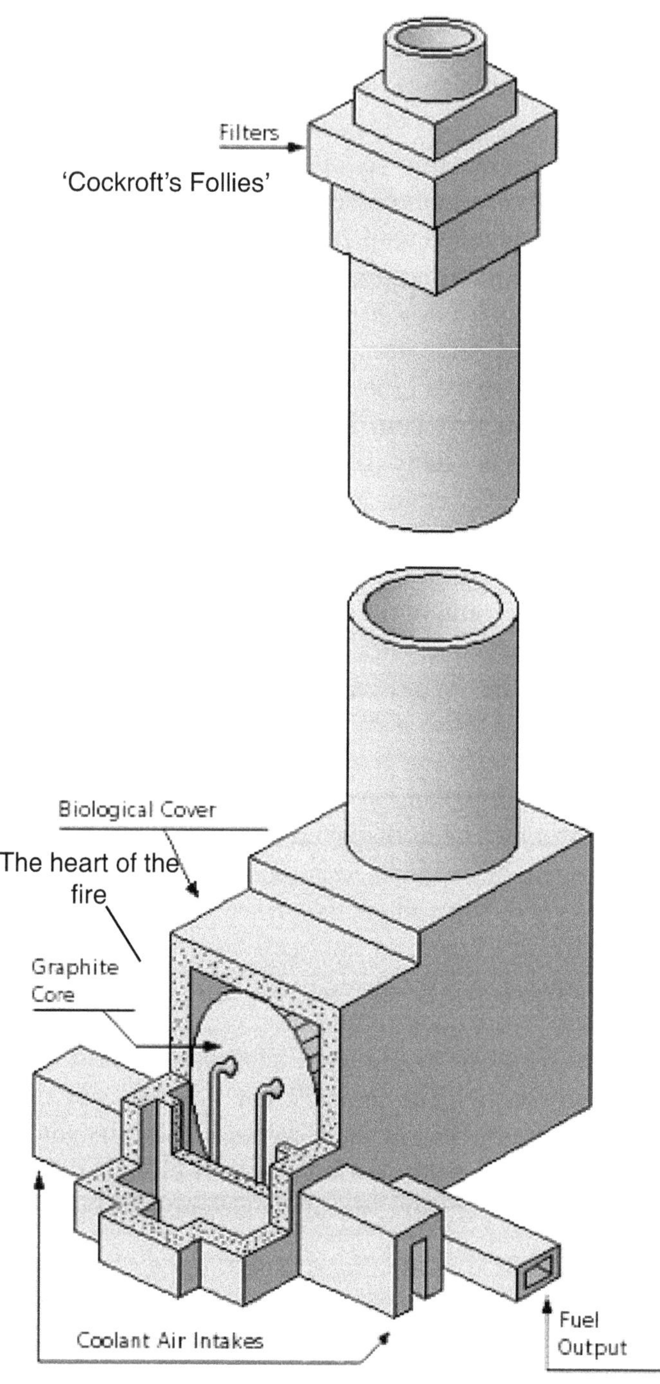

Cutaway diagram of Windscale reactor.
Image courtesy HereToHelp on Wikipedia

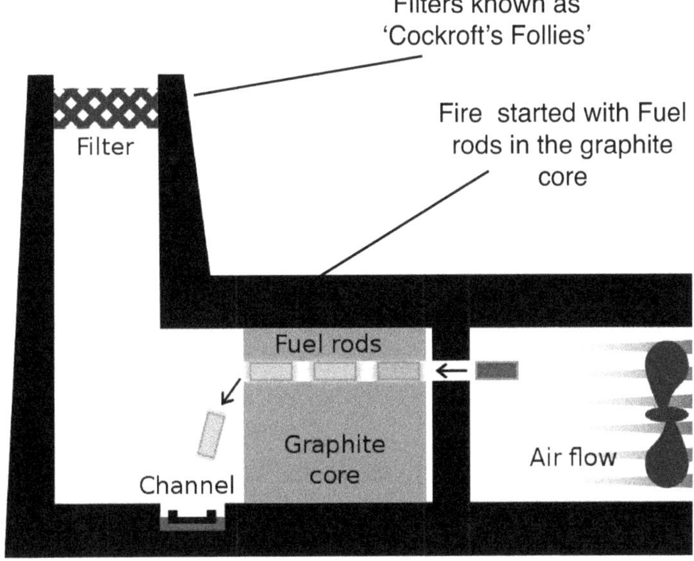

The design of Windscale Pile No. 1, with one of the many fuel channels illustrated. The fire occurred in this section of the reactor.

Image courtesy HereToHelp on Wikipedia

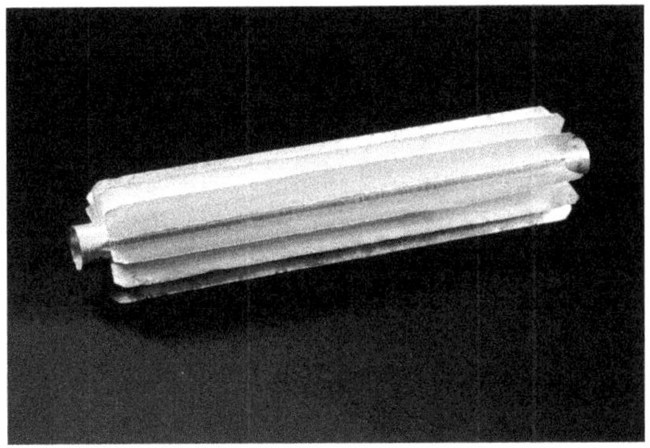

Finned aluminium canister containing uranium fuel for The Windscale Reactor

Sources

Thomas Tuohy Obituary *The Independent* 26th March 2008
Windscale: Britain's Biggest Nuclear Disaster BBC 2007
'The Penney Report' Official enquiry into the Windscale Fire 17th to 25th October 1957

Chapter 8
The Day They Dropped The Bomb

At the height of the Cold War in the 1950s, the backbone of the United States' defence against attack by the Soviet Union was the Strategic Air Command. This force was largely manned by B-36, B-47 and B-52 bombers armed with thermonuclear weapons. A typical payload would be between two and four nuclear bombs. These aircraft would alternate on long distance missions from their bases in the United States to the edge of the Iron Curtain from the Arctic to the Caucasus. The missions would have codenames such as *Head Start, Chrome Dome, Hard Head* and *Round Robin*.

Inevitably, there were accidents and aircraft were lost. This chapter deals with the numerous accidents during this period in which nuclear armed USAF aircraft were involved. In a significant number of cases, a nuclear bomb was either lost or destroyed. The US military have an apt name for such aerial and other nuclear accidents, they are called Broken Arrows.

The First Broken Arrow
USAF B-36 Peacemaker Crash
Mount Kologet, British Columbia
14th February 1950

On a bitterly cold day on 13th February 1950, a Convair B-36 *Peacemaker* bomber took off from Eielson Air Force Base near Fairbanks in Alaska. Known as Bomber Number 075, the plane was on a 6,000 mile training mission starting and terminating at Carswell Air Force Base near Fort Worth, Texas. The initial leg was a 3,000 mile journey from the Texas base to Fairbanks, Alaska. From there, 075 would travel south keeping out of Canadian air space.

Flying down the Pacific seaboard, the plane was due to make a mock nuclear attack on San Francisco that would unknowingly double as the Russian city of Leningrad (now St Petersburg). An important part of this training mission was to test the crew's capabilities under extreme weather conditions. Number 075 was one of ten other B-36s on this mission and the ninth aircraft to take off.

As well as the 15 regular crew on board, the plane carried a a weaponeer and a bomb commander. These two additional crew members were present to arm the Mark IV atomic bomb on board the B-36. At this early stage of the Cold War the American military were still refining the arming procedure on their airborne nuclear weapons. So, practising this process was also an important part of 075's training mission. For safety reasons, nuclear weapons on board bombers were always only armed once the aircraft had taken off. Usually, the arming process would take place on approach to the actual target.

Even today, it remains unclear whether this B-36 was actually carrying a real plutonium core which would provide the trigger for the bomb or a lead dummy for training purposes. Either way, the bomb itself did have a substantial amount natural uranium and 5,000 lbs of conventional explosives on board. This brought its total weight up to 11,000 lbs.

One of the many extraordinary aspects of this whole incident was that, at this time the United States Air Force did not have ownership of any nuclear bombs. Then, all the nuclear bombs in the U.S. were owned by the Atomic Energy Commission. Since the AEC was a civilian rather than military organisation, this seems a very strange arrangement. The Mark IV bomb on board B-36 number 075 had been loaned by the AEC to the USAF specifically for this exercise.

The ground temperature at Fairbanks when the B-36 took off was -40 C which started a build up of ice in the aircraft's engines. As the flight progressed, the crew experienced problems contacting their operational base; because of this, all radio communications had to be relayed via the nearest B-36 number 083 which was in the same vicinity as 075.

During the pre-flight briefing, the crews of all ten B-36s had been warned of expect severe icing conditions en route. If these conditions were encountered, they were ordered to climb above the weather to avoid the engines icing up and failing.

At 11:25 p.m., 075 was at an altitude of 12,000 feet when a serious build up of ice on the wings and engines started. The accumulation of ice on the carburettors of the B-36's engines began to cause them to seriously malfunction. The plane's commander, Captain H. L. Barry, ordered it to climb to 15,000 feet to escape these icy conditions. Almost immediately after this, engine number one caught fire. Then engines two and five also caught fire and had to be feathered. With the loss of half its six prop engines, the B-36 began to lose height rapidly. At this stage, the plane's location was close to both Queen Charlotte and Vancouver Islands in what is known as the Inside Channel which runs down the northern coast of British Columbia, Canada.

Realising the plane could not remain airborne on half its prop engines, Captain Barry made the fateful decision for the crew to abandon the aircraft. Whilst the rest of the crew struggled into their survival gear and parachutes, the plane's weaponeer Ted Schreier was disarming the Mark IV bomb. Whether he had time to fully complete this task is unknown since he did not survive the crash. This was the last any of the crew saw of the weaponeer and none of them recalled seeing Shreier bail out of the B-36.

Just before the crew bailed out, the bomb commander ordered the weapon to be dropped to explode about 3,800 feet above the waters of Queen Charlotte Sound. At least one crew member recalled seeing and hearing the subsequent explosion.

Apparently, the crew had been ordered to bail out when the B-36 was at an altitude of 5,000 feet over Princess Royal Island. Just before bailing out Captain Barry set the autopilot for the aircraft to fly out over the Pacific and ditch safely away from land. With the plane losing height at 200-500 feet per minute it should not have been more than ten minutes before the plane crashed into the sea. The dark shape of the pilotless B-36 gently banking in the night sky was the last the surviving crew would ever see of their aircraft as they parachuted towards the ground. The time was just past 12:00 a.m. on Valentine's Day, February 14th 1950.

The last message from B-36 075 was just before the crew bailed out around midnight on February 13th/14th. It was a mayday alert that the plane was going down. This immediately sparked a massive sea and air search with emergency response units being activated across a wide area surrounding the Pacific Coasts of Canada and the U.S. Called Operation Brix, it was the largest U.S./Canadian rescue operation of its time. Within minutes of that last distress call, large numbers of Canadian and American personnel, aircraft and rescue vessels began gravitating towards the last point of contact of the B-36. Given it is a vast area of rugged coastline and wild mountainous land, it could not have been an easy search.

There had been a report of a large aircraft overflying Vancouver Island and it was thought this was one of the last sightings of 075. As a result, Operation Brix concentrated the search on that area. Only later would it be evident that the aircraft in question had been the B-36's sister aircraft number 083.

On the afternoon of 15th February 1950 the crew of fishing vessel *Cape Perry* spotted and rescued the first two members of the surviving bomber crew on Princess Royal Island. They then spotted a third survivor and shortly afterwards seven more crew. By the third day of Operation Brix, two more air crew had been found alive, but the remaining five crew including Schreier were never found. At this time no trace of the B-36 itself with its A-bomb was located. Once the crew bailed out it had literally vanished off the radar.

The search was then scaled down. It was assumed that the five missing crew had died of hypothermia having parachuted into frigid waters of the Pacific. It was also assumed that the B-36 had ditched into the sea. Very soon the world's attention was diverted away to a much bigger story - the outbreak of the Korean War. It is safe to say that the top brass of USAF were not entirely sorry about this. The loss of one of their state of the art bombers with a borrowed nuclear weapon on board had been an acute embarrassment not to mention the tragic loss of life.

For the next three and a half years, the loss of B-36 number 075 was all but forgotten by the world's media. Then in the autumn of 1953, the search for another missing aircraft unearthed a remarkable find. This time the search was for a De Havilland Dove with oil millionaire Ellis Hall and his family on board. The plane had vanished whilst flying between Annette Island in Alaska and Bellingham in Washington State. On 3rd September 1953, one of the 26 search aircraft spotted the wreckage of B-36 Number 075 on a glacier on the slopes of Mount Kologet at an altitude of 6,000 feet. **(1)**

This discovery posed a number of intriguing questions about both the B-36 and its crash location. Firstly, Captain Barry had set the autopilot to fly the plane out into the Pacific Ocean where it could crash safely. So, how was it possible that the B-36 had flown inland in the opposite direction for three hours before crashing on a mountainside glacier? Secondly, the crew had abandoned the plane when the loss of three engines meant it could no longer stay in the air. If that was the case how had the aircraft then climbed to an altitude of of well over 12,000 feet to avoid the mountains before crashing at an altitude of 6,000 feet on Mount Kologet lying beyond this range? Thirdly, the rescue plane had identified the B-36 from its markings. Some of these were the numbers 511 on the nose wheel door. These numbers could only have been seen if that door had been opened to allow the undercarriage to be lowered for landing. How was this possible in an aircraft flying on autopilot without any crew on board? Or had someone flown the B-36 to its final destination?

Once the missing B-36 had been located, the U.S. authorities were naturally keen to retrieve the most security sensitive items on board. Most important of these were the Mark IV A-bomb and its plutonium core, if indeed they were still on the aircraft.

Although it was thought the actual bomb had been ditched out to sea, the authorities needed to make absolutely certain it was not still on the aircraft. There was also the strong possibility that the plutonium core of the bomb *could* still be in the wreckage. Not only was this core very valuable it was also highly dangerous with the potential for flattening Mt Kologet if it exploded. However, reaching the wreck to retrieve the core was easier said than done.

As well was the crash location being very remote and inaccessible, the weather was also terrible. So, it took the U.S. search teams four attempts to actually reach it. Once there, they removed some highly sensitive equipment before blowing up what remained of the wrecked *Peacemaker*. Whether they found the plutonium core remains shrouded in secrecy. There are also two other big question marks over the U.S. team's activities at the crash site. The first is whether they found the remains of one of the missing crewmen aboard the aircraft.

Due to their knowledge of the mountainous terrain, the Americans enlisted some of the ranchers living in the area to help in their search. These people were adamant that the remains of one of the missing crew members was removed from the aircraft in the 1954 expedition. This seems to be backed up by an official document that has subsequently come to light stating that a body was removed from the crash. If this was the case, was it the remains of the B-36's mystery pilot?

The second question is why the U.S. team blew up the wreckage of Bomber 075? In the past, other B-36s that crashed in remote places had simply been left in place. So why was this one singled out for specially destructive treatment?

These and many other details of this search and destroy mission are still secret all these years later. However, in his fascinating book '*Lost Nuke - The Last Flight of Bomber 075*' (2) Dirk Septer presents a convincing and detailed theory as to how B-36 crashed on a Canadian mountain and not the Pacific. Septer believes that the weaponeer Captain Theodore Schreier did not bail out of the B-36, but actually flew it inland. Why would he do that? The answer could be that he was well aware of the importance and value of the plutonium core which he had removed from the bomb. Was he attempting to fly the plane to a location where this heart of the nuclear weapon was out of the reach of hostile forces?

A discovery Septer made on a visit to the crash site with a documentary film crew lends weight to his theory. On that occasion, he found a parachute in perfect condition pointing to the fact that one of the crew members did not actually jump. Was it feasible that one person would be able to fly the stricken B-36 in the middle of a winter's night for more than 3 hours over high mountains?

In the case of Shreier, Septer believes the answer is yes. The weaponeer's extensive experience as a combat pilot in the Second World War would have been sufficient to enable him to fly the B-36 on his own. However, this raises another important question. Assuming Ted Schreier was at the controls of B-36 number 075 how was he able to climb to an altitude of 12,000 feet with the plane firing on only three engines? Had he been able to restart the other three engines? Perhaps, or maybe he used the four booster jets to climb over the mountains. These were normally only used to aid takeoff but could have helped the plane to increase altitude and stay in the air.

The warmer land temperatures could also have caused the ice to slide off the wings thereby reducing the weight of the aircraft. This would also have helped it to increase altitude.

These many questions and theories about the last flight of B-36 075 are likely to stay unanswered. This is partly because so much secrecy still surrounds its ultimate discovery and destruction by the U.S. Forces. So, it is likely that the last flight of *Peacemaker* Number 075 will remain one of most enduring mysteries of The Cold War.

Footnotes

1 On 6th September 1953, the search for Ellis Hall's aircraft was officially ended. The aircraft was eventually found a month later by a local pilot called Herman Ludwigsen. The wreckage was scattered over a wide area indicating that it had broken up in flight. Sadly there were no survivors.

2 *Lost Nuke - The Last Flight of Bomber 075* By Dirk Septer Heritage House Publishers ISBN Number 978-1-926936-87-1

B-36 '*Peacemaker*' nuclear bomber similar to the one that crashed under mysterious circumstances on Mount Kologet in British Columbia, Canada in February 1950.
Photograph courtesy USAF

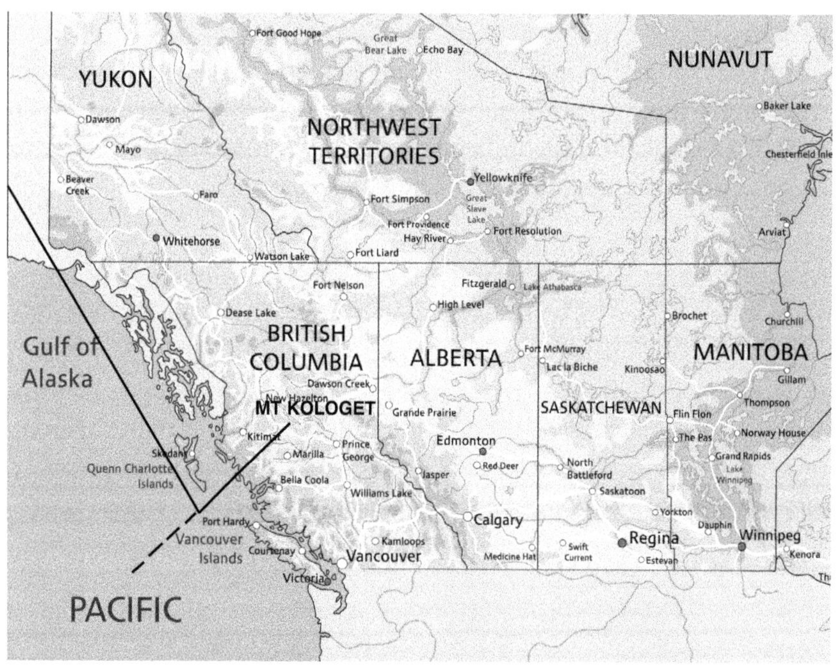

Map of the last flight of B-36 *Peacemaker* No 075
Unbroken line shows route down Pacific seaboard of US and Canada and then 'pilotless' inland to Mt Kologet. Broken line shows the route the plane should have taken on autopilot.

Two Identical Broken Arrows
The New Mexico and Idaho Crashes
11th April and 13th July 1950

One of the USAF's golden rules for carrying nuclear weapons in their planes was that these bombs were never armed until after the aircraft had taken off. This was a safety measure to ensure these weapons did not detonate in the event of a crash.

Two forceful and tragic reminders of this rule occurred early in the Cold War on April and July 1950. At just after 9:30 in the evening of 11th April, a B-29 Superfortress bomber lifted off the ground at Kirtland Air Force Base near Albuquerque in New Mexico. On board the giant aircraft was an A-bomb, its detonators and plutonium core for triggering the weapon. Three minutes later something went badly wrong and the plane ploughed into the ground at Manzano Base, a top secret nuclear facility adjoining Kirtland AFB. The plane exploded in a massive fireball which also ignited the high explosives in the A-bomb destroying its protective casing and scattering fragments across the wreckage.

As the bomb was not armed with crucial components such as detonators and trigger core, a nuclear detonation was averted. These components were subsequently recovered intact. Tragically all thirteen crew members died in the crash.

Three months later on 13th July 1950, an almost identical accident destroyed a B-50 Superfortress in a crash in rural Wright County, Ohio. On this occasion the B-50, which was a variation of the B-29, had taken off from Briggs Air Force Base in Texas to fly to a base in the UK. The flight included a stopover at Wright-Patterson Air Base at Dayton, Ohio. On board was an unarmed nuclear weapon, possibly a Mark IV A-bomb.

Whilst flying at 7,000 feet in clear weather the plane suddenly nosed down and crashed. On this occasion whilst the bomb had no triggering core, the high explosives within the weapon exploded on hitting the ground. All sixteen crew members perished in the accident.

Despite a lengthy investigation by USAF, Boeing, the aircraft manufacturer and Pratt & Witney who made the engines, no definite cause for the crash could be found. This was mainly due to the total destruction of the plane on impact.

One possible clue was the account of eyewitness Clive Schutts from the nearby town of Lebanon. He described hearing one of the plane's engines racing and seeing the aircraft spiralling towards the ground. Other eyewitnesses also said they saw the plane in a spiral before hitting the ground. Whilst eyewitness accounts can be notoriously contradictory and unreliable, in the absence of material evidence, these possibly point to engine malfunction.

The California B-29 Crash
Fairfield Suisan (Travis) AFB, California
5th August 1950

On 25th June 1950, the Korean War started with thousands of troops spilling over the border from the Communist North. U.S. President Truman, afraid that South Korea's President Singman Rhee would make good on his promise to invade the North had kept the South Korean army chronically short of weapons and resources. As a result, the South Korean Army was quickly overwhelmed by the Communist invaders.

Within weeks, a United Nations Force led by the United States was fighting the North Korean People's Army on the peninsula. In those first few weeks and months things did not go well for the UN side which quickly found itself with its back to the wall. It was at this time that many in the upper echelons of the U.S. Government and military considered the possibility of using nuclear weapons in the conflict.

Against this backdrop ten nuclear armed B-29 bombers were despatched to Guam in the Pacific. The purpose of this was twofold: to deter Mao Zedong's Communist Chinese Government from invading Taiwan and the possible use of nuclear weapons in Korea. The codenames for these aircraft were *Silverplates*.

At ten o'clock on the evening of 5th August 1950, one of these ten B-29s took off from Fairfield Suisan Air Force Base in California to make the 5,816 miles journey to Guam. On board were 20 passengers and crew and a Mark IV nuclear bomb. Initially all was well, with all the engines turning at 2,800 rpm. Three quarters of the way down the 8,000 foot runway, engine two went rogue with its props suddenly spinning at 3,500 rpm.

Ordering this engine to be feathered, Captain Eugene Steffes managed to take off. Unfortunately, engine three then started to race dangerously with its props also spinning at 3,500 rpm. To compound the aircraft's problems, the undercarriage also jammed and would not retract. This reduced the aircraft's speed from 155 mph to 145 mph. Realising this was not fast enough to clear the terrain beyond the runway, Steffes initiated a crash landing close to a trailer park.

Hitting the ground at 120 mph, the B-29 broke in two and burst into flames. Police and a firefighting crew were quickly on the scene as were the four workers in the Air Base bakery led by Sergeant Lewis Siqueira. When it became clear the blaze was intensifying and they were unable to help any further, Siqueira ordered his workers back to a safe distance. Unable to ignore the cries for help coming from the crashed aircraft, one of them, Sgt Ramoneda, turned back to help. It was a decision that would cost him his life.

Less than half an hour after the plane had come down the blaze ignited the high explosives on the Mark IV nuclear bomb. This secondary explosion engulfed an area of two square miles. Nineteen of the crew perished along with seven people on the ground including Ramoneda and five firefighters.

The subsequent enquiry found that the malfunction in engine two that led to the crash was due to faulty maintenance. Since the other engine number three and its props were never found, a similar conclusion could not be drawn. No fault was found in the undercarriage mechanism that caused Captain Steffes so much trouble.

Fortunately, the A-bomb on board the B-29 was not armed at the time thus preventing a conventional explosion 'going nuclear.' It is not known how much of this weapon was salvable. It was not until 44 years later in 1994 that it was officially acknowledged this bomber was carrying a nuclear weapon.

Among those killed in this tragic crash was World War Two veteran Brigadier General Robert F. Travis. On 20th October 1950 Fairfield Suisan Air Force Base was renamed Travis in his honour. An official renaming ceremony was held on 20th April 1951 with members of the Travis family in attendance and presided over by Earl Warren, The Governor of California at the time.

Sources

'Seconds spell great tragedy in B-29 crash'. Spokane Daily Chronicle. (Washington). Associated Press. 7th August 1950.

A-Bomb Explosion over the St Lawrence
Rivière-du-Loup, Quebec, Canada
10th November 1950

The sleepy little town of Rivière-du-Loup, lies on the St Lawrence River about 300 miles north of the Canadian city of Montreal. It is the sort of place where the locals boast that "nothing ever happens here". That all changed on 10th November 1950 when a USAF B-50 Superfortress developed engine trouble 10,500 feet above the town. The plane was ferrying an unprimed Mark IV A-bomb from Goose Air Force Base in Labrador back to the United States at the time.

Becoming concerned his plane would not make it to their scheduled destination, the captain made preparations for an emergency landing. As per standing orders, he instructed the crew to jettison the bomb over the St Lawrence River. The high explosives within the A-bomb casing exploded at 2,500 feet as primed by the crew. It was not a nuclear blast of course, but to the residents of Rivière-du-Loup it seemed that way. The huge bang was heard throughout the area, rattling windows and terrifying inhabitants and livestock.

Later, the U.S. military authorities explained that the explosion had been caused by a conventional 500 lb practice bomb. It was not until thirty years later that the authorities 'came clean' and admitted that the true cause of the blast was the Mk IV A-Bomb. Even though it was unarmed, the weapon had contained 100 lbs of depleted uranium that was scattered like confetti over Rivière-du-Loup and the St Lawrence River.

Boeing B-50 similar to the one that dropped the bomb on Rivière-du-Loup.
Photograph courtesy USAF

Into Thin Air
The Mysterious Disappearance of B-47 Stratojet number 52-534
Mediterranean Sea
10th March 1956

In the spring of 1956, a B-47E Stratojet bomber took off from McDill Air base in Florida to make the long journey to Ben Guerir in Morocco. During the Cold War such long non-stop flights were routine for SAC planes and their crews and included two refuelling rendezvous.

The B-47 was carrying a precious cargo of two plutonium cores for triggering nuclear weapons. As plutonium is so dangerously radioactive, these cores were placed in protective lead cases aboard the aircraft.

The flight was uneventful until arrival over the Mediterranean Sea. At that point the Captain of the B-47, Robert H. Hodgin, guided his plane down through thick cloud to meet up with the second refuelling tanker at 14,000 feet. It was then that the giant bomber, its crew and precious cargo vanished forever.

The rendezvous with the refuelling aircraft was never kept and the aircraft did not send out any distress signal. The air/sea rescue search found no trace of any wreckage or bodies floating in the sea. The actual crash site of the aircraft has never been located.

A French news agency reported that the plane *might have* exploded in the vicinity of the coastal town of Sebatna in what is now Algeria. This was an approximate match to the last position of the aircraft calculated by USAF being 90 miles to the South West of Oran, Algeria. In spite of the extensive search by the French military and Royal Naval vessels nothing was found.

The disappearance of B-47 Stratojet number 52-534 remains one of the Cold War's most enduring mysteries.

Sources

Narrative Summaries of Accidents Involving U.S. Nuclear Weapons 1950-80

U.S. Department of Defense.

Air Safety Network report # 60616

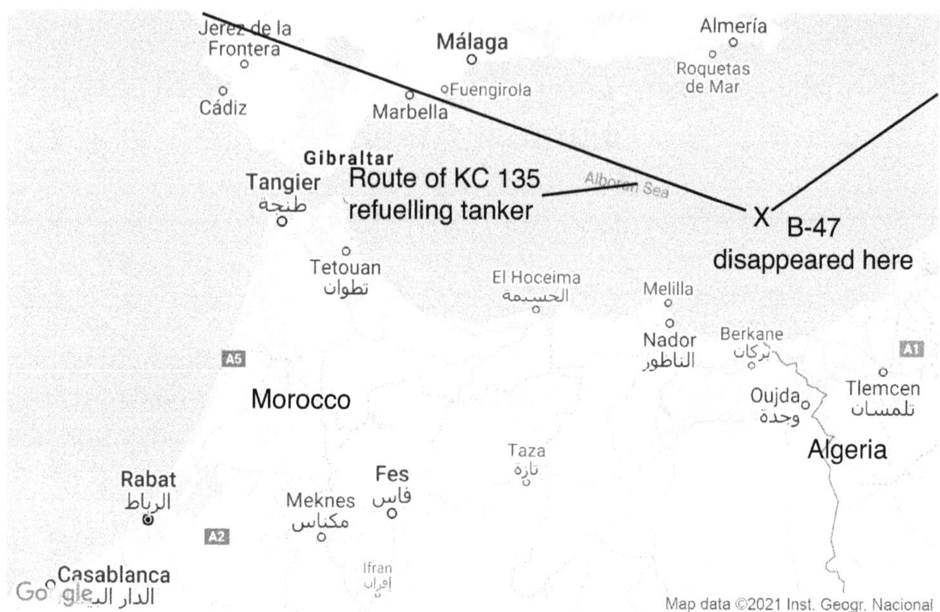

Map showing approximate disappearance location of B-47 Stratojet number 52-534

B-47 Stratojet similar to the one that disappeared off North Africa in 1956

A Triple Nuclear Accident RAF Lakenheath, Suffolk, England 27th July 1956

One of the more alarming nuclear accidents of the Cold War happened in the depths of rural England. Lakenheath in Suffolk has long been an important NATO and USAF air base. In the summer of 1956, B-47 Stratojets of Strategic Air Command were flying in and out of there on a daily basis. Much of their flying time was taken up with training flights. This was to ensure the crews and their planes were in a state of maximum readiness and proficiency twenty-four hours a day.

On 27th July of that year, B-47E Stratojet number 53-4230 piloted by Captain Russell Bowling was returning to Lakenheath after completing a bombing training mission. As the plane touched down, it fell foul of a notorious ‘hump’ in the runway. This rise in the land over which the runway was constructed was well known to the crews of the B-47s stationed at Lakenheath. Since it accentuated the B-47’s tendency to ‘porpoise’ or bounce on landing they were sure that one day a touch down would end in disaster for a Stratojet.

On that fateful summer’s day just such a disaster overtook Bowling’s B-47. As luck would have it, the plane touched down on the actual hump causing the plane to ‘porpoise’. As the B-47’s wheels remade contact with the runway it bounced again and its right wing struck the ground. This caused the plane to flip to the left where that wing also hit the ground hard.

Now out of control, the big jet left the runway and bounced across the grass hitting a storage igloo containing three Mark VI nuclear bombs. Although these weapons were not armed with plutonium cores they did contain a significant amount of high explosives. One of the bombs also had detonators fitted. These were sheared off in the accident. The fact that they did not explode was later described as ‘a miracle’ by one explosives expert. Fortunately, the fire caused by the accident also failed to ignite the explosives within the bomb casings.

By chance, this flight had an extra man on board in addition to the three regular crew. He was Technical Sergeant John Ulrich who was on the flight to check some issues with the plane’s electronics. Tragically, neither he nor the rest of the crew survived the crash.

It seems such landings and take offs were filmed for training purposes. As a result, a ten minute film of this awful crash and its aftermath survives and can be seen on You Tube.

In January 1961, RAF Lakenheath experienced another nuclear scare. This one involved an F-100 Super Sabre jet fighter that was armed with a Mark 28 H-bomb. As the pilot turned on the aircraft's engines, he accidentally released the aircraft's fuel tanks. The impact on the concrete apron caused the aviation fuel in the tanks to ignite, engulfing the fighter and the nuclear bomb in flames. Fortunately prompt action by the emergency services ensured that the high explosives in the H-bomb did not explode. The pilot survived the accident.

It was only later that it was discovered that a fault in the wiring mechanism of the Mark 28 bomb could have allowed heat to cirumvent the safety systems thereby triggering a nuclear explosion of a 70 kiloton bomb. The consequences of such an explosion on Eastern England and beyond would have been truly catastrophic.

Dropped By Mistake
Kirtland Air Force Base, New Mexico, United States
27th May 1957

In the spring of 1957 a strange accident occurred at Kirtland Air Force Base in New Mexico. The facts are that a B-36 was coming in to land at the base when it dropped the Mark 17 thermonuclear bomb it was carrying. Some accounts say that the bomb actually tore loose from its cradle and broke through the closed bomb doors. Others describe the release simply as 'unintentional'.

As the plane was only 1,700 feet above the ground, the parachute on the weapon was not deployed. The impact with the ground triggered the high explosives in the bomb completely destroying it and leaving a crater 25 feet wide and 12 feet deep. Although the weapon was not armed with its plutonium core at the time of the accident, radioactive material contaminated a one mile area around the point of impact.

Mercifully, the bomb fell on a cow pasture just south of the base and not on an inhabited area of nearby Albuquerque. The military authorities did a thorough clean up of the accident site removing all traces of the bomb debris and radioactive soil. In the absence of any further details, questions remain about just how this bomb came to be dropped so close to the B-36 landing in the first place.

In 1996, The Center For Land Use Interpretation placed a marker identifying the spot where the Mark 17 bomb landed. The CLUI is a non profit body *'dedicated to the increase in knowledge about how the nation's lands are apportioned, utilised and perceived.'* This involves identifying sites of interest in the United States landscape such as the Mark 17 accident. However, this marker has since been removed. Why this was done and who removed it is a mystery. One answer could be that it was done by the authorities who wanted any reminder of this embarrassing incident removed from the public memory.

The Mystery of The Tybee Bomb
Tybee Island,Georgia, United States
5th February 1958

Tybee is a small island just off the Georgia coast about 18 miles from the city of Savannah. With its attractive old lighthouse and a history stretching back to the Spanish occupation in the sixteenth century, the island is a popular tourist and yachting destination.

This seemingly idyllic spot also harbours a dark modern mystery that worries many of the locals. At two a.m. on a February night in 1958 a United States Air Force B-47 Stratojet was flying over the Georgia mainland at an altitude of 38000 feet.

Piloted by Colonel Howard Richardson, the plane was on a top secret combat training mission out of the aircraft's home base at Homestead AFB in Florida. On board was a truly formidable Mark 15 thermonuclear bomb. Weighing 7,600 lbs (3,400 kg) it had the power to flatten any city on earth many times over.

Richardson's plane was accompanied by a second B-47 on this simulated combat mission. To increase the realism of the exercise, F-86 Sabre fighter jets were scrambled to make a mock attack on the B-47s. It was at this point, something went badly wrong. For some reason the radar on one of the fighters did not "see" Richardson's B-47 and sliced through one of its wings. The collision tore the left wing off the F-86 and sent the *Stratojet* into a terrifying 18,000 foot uncontrolled dive. The pilot of the fighter Lt Clarence Stewart ejected and survived, landing in a swamp.

Thanks to the skill of Colonel Richardson, the B-47 was finally brought under control at 20,000 feet. With one of the bomber's engines missing Richardson realised he had to make an emergency landing. To do this safely, he knew he had to eject the nuclear weapon to avoid the possibility of it exploding during what promised to be a bumpy landing. Once over the sea off the Georgia coast the crew released their deadly cargo. It landed in the deep silt on the sea bed close to Tybee Island. It was probably this that cushioned the impact and prevented the conventional high explosives encased in the bomb from detonating.

Colonel Richardson then made an emergency landing at nearby Hunter Air Force Base. He was awarded the Distinguished Flying Cross for saving both the stricken bomber and its crew.

The US military began their search for the bomb on February 6th 1958. It was a big joint operation involving the USAF's specialist 2700th Explosive Ordnance Disposal Squadron and a hundred Navy personnel. In spite of the fact the searchers knew the bomb had fallen somewhere in a four square mile area of shallow water known as Wassaw Sound off Tybee Island they were unable to find it. Even their array of sophisticated search equipment could find no trace of the lost weapon.

On 16th April the search was called off. Since then, there have been numerous unofficial searches but the Mark 15 bomb remains stubbornly hidden in the sea off Tybee Island.

One of these searches was conducted by Lt Colonel Derek Duke (USAF Retired) in 2004. He found abnormally high radiation readings of an area known as Little Tybee Island. Following this, the Air Force authorities made a search of the area and concluded that the radiation Lt. Colonel Duke picked up was from a locally occurring mineral called monazite. Perhaps they are right and Duke was mistaken. By the same token, could they be wrong. So, could he have found the missing bomb?

One reason why the bomb has proved so difficult to find could be because it is actually embedded much deeper in the ground than anyone thinks. In fact, the weight and velocity of the falling bomb might have caused it to burrow into the earth many metres below the soft layer of silt on the sea bed. This would not only defeat the most sophisticated sonar devices it would also help contain radioactive leakages.

Another area of controversy is whether the bomb was armed with its plutonium trigger when it was jettisoned from the B-47. If so, the residents of Georgia and Tybee Island face the alarming prospect of a fully primed H -Bomb sitting on their doorstep. The US Air Force has always maintained that the plutonium trigger had been removed from the bomb before that fateful flight. If that was the case it would have been in accordance with the Air Force's own safety rules when transporting nuclear weapons.

However, this was apparently contradicted in 1966 by Assistant Secretary of Defense, W J Howard when he testified to Congress. He stated that the lost Tybee bomb was *'a complete weapon, a bomb with a nuclear capsule'*. It was, he added, one of only two nuclear weapons that had been lost with their plutonium core triggers in place.*

The Georgia Department of Natural Resources have been unable to detect any abnormal levels of radioactivity in the area where the Tybee bomb is believed to be buried. This is not what one would expect if a fully primed H-bomb was in the vicinity. If, as was previously speculated, the bomb is much deeper in the ground, this could account for the absence of high radiation.

However, even if the bomb is not armed with a plutonium trigger, it contains sufficient conventional explosives and uranium to make quite a mess if it exploded.

**The other lost bomb that W.J.Howard referred to was probably a nuclear weapon that sank in the Philippines Sea in 1965. On that occasion, a Douglas Skyhawk A4 fighter carrying a B 43 nuclear bomb was being transferred from a hangar bay to an elevator on the aircraft carrier USS Ticonderoga. While this was happening the aircraft accidentally fell over the side. The pilot Lt Douglas Webster, the A4 Fighter and the bomb all sank to a depth of 19,000 feet in the Philippines Sea.*

At the time, the US military authorities said that the accident happened 500 miles from the nearest point of land. It was twenty or so years later that the US Government admitted that the carrier had been as close as 80 miles from the Japanese Ryukyu Islands. When this was made public it caused widespread outrage in Japan sparking a diplomatic incident with the United States.

Mark 15 H-bomb similar to the one jettisoned from the damaged B-47 Stratojet over Wassaw Sound, Tybee Island, Georgia, U.S.
Photograph US Government

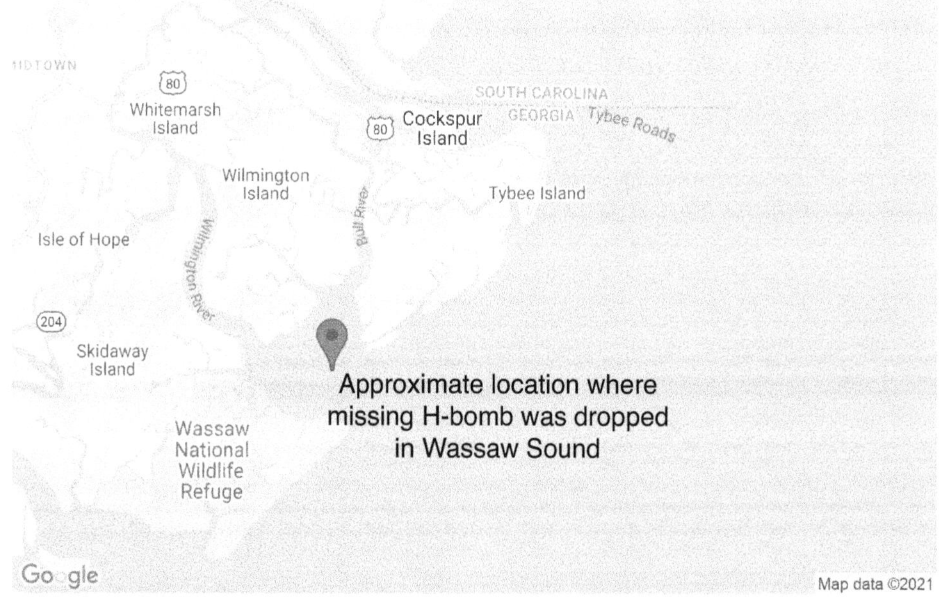

Wassaw Sound with Tybee Island just to the North.
Map created by Nick Brazil using Google Template

Boeing B-47 Stratojet similar to the aircraft involved in the Tybee Island bomb incident.
Photograph USAF

F-86 Sabre similar to the aircraft involved in the Tybee Island bomb incident.
Photograph USAF

The Greenham Common Accident
RAF Greenham Common
28th February 1958

On a cold and very windy day in February 1958, a B-47 Stratofortress was lining up for takeoff at the end of the long runway at RAF Greenham Common near the Berkshire market town of Newbury in Southern England. Following closure as a Second World War air base in the late 1940s Greenham Common had been reactivated during the early years of the Cold War as a joint RAF/USAF Base.

Its new role was a base for nuclear bombers of the U.S. Strategic Air Command in countering the Soviet threat. Armed with nuclear weapons the B-47 waiting for takeoff on that February day in 1958 was part of one of these SAC patrols. At 4:25 p.m. the bomber was cleared for takeoff. What happened immediately after that has been a matter of dispute and interpretation ever since. The basic facts are that almost immediately after take off the B-47 developed unspecified control difficulties and was ordered to jettison its two 1,700 gallon wing tanks in a safe impact zone by the runway. Unfortunately, the tanks missed their target with one of them igniting 65 feet from another B-47 which was parked up for refuelling. This bomber, which was allegedly carrying a 1.1 megaton nuclear bomb, was engulfed in flames. The other fuel tank hit a hangar wall and also exploded.

Due to the large amount of flammable magnesium used in the construction of the B-47, the plane burned fiercely taking a total of 16 hours and a million gallons of water to put it out. Two US service personnel were killed and a further eight were injured in the accident.

It has always been alleged that this accident was considerably more serious than admitted. According to the British anti nuclear group The Campaign for Nuclear Disarmament (CND), the whole incident was covered up for over 30 years. This allegation was also repeated in the short article about the accident in Wikipedia. Furthermore, the generally accurate account of the incident unearthed by CND also alleges that the conflagration spread a high level of radiation around the base and the surrounding area.

"The bomb burned, releasing deadly uranium and plutonium oxide powder over an area of several miles around the base. The conventional explosive in the warhead exploded, helping to scatter very fine uranium and plutonium particles."

Is this what really happened?

Interestingly, in 2017 the BBC interviewed Gordon Smith who worked as a civilian electrician at the base in 1958. He was an eyewitness to the accident and remembered one of the jettisoned fuel tanks dropping through the roof of a hangar and destroying a B-47 which was being serviced there.

Mr. Smith also asserted that the bomber was not armed. We do not know how he knew this, but if the plane was being serviced it is doubtful it would be armed at the time. If this is what happened, it would nullify any assertions by CND or anyone else that there was widespread radiation from the accident. It is also interesting that this eyewitness placed the destroyed aircraft in a maintenance hangar - an entirely different location to all the other reports on the crash.

The account in the documents discovered by the CND in 1996 also refer to radiation being spread by conventional explosives in the nuclear weapons on board the destroyed B-47. These explosives are built into nuclear weapons to destroy the multiple triggering devices on the bombs thus preventing a full scale nuclear blast in the event of an accident. It is therefore unlikely although not impossible that these conventional explosives would release any radiation from the weapons. The CND documents also refer to the bomb burning and releasing radiation. It has to be said that in all the cases of nuclear weapons being on board aircraft crashing there has not been one incident of the nuclear weapons they were carrying actually catching fire.

The CND document also referred to a statement by two scientists from the nearby Atomic Weapons Research Establishmen at Aldermaston. They stated that in 1961 they discovered high concentrations of radiation around Greenham Common Air Base.

In 1997, Newbury District Council commissioned a seven month long survey by the Geosciences Advisory Unit of Southampton University to establish whether or not there was significant radiation around the former air base at Greenham Common. At the end of this search, this team was unable to uncover any significant amounts of radiation in the area. From this they concluded there was no evidence of a nuclear accident having occurred at the base.

Finally, the allegation that the whole accident had been covered up for thirty years, is also problematic. This is because *Hansard* 5th March 1958 records that a Government minister, a Mr Ward M.P. gave a fairly full account of the accident in the Houses of Parliament. (*See Appendix 2)*

This was in the form of a Parliamentary answer to a question about the accident raised by Anthony Hurd, the M.P. for Newbury. It should be pointed out that in his statement the Minister made no mention of any nuclear weapons being involved in the accident. This may have been for security and political reasons or simply because there were no such weapons on the aircraft in the first place.

Whatever the full truth of the Greenham Common accident, questions and allegations of a 'cover up' will remain. If the B-47 destroyed by fire was being refuelled on the runway at the time, it is likely it would have been armed with nuclear weapons. This needs to be balanced against the eyewitness account by the electrician Gordon Smith saying that there was no bomb on board the aircraft. This also seems to be born out by the Southampton University survey not finding any significant radiation at Greenham.

The apparent disparity in Gordon Smith's eyewitness account and the official account relating to the location of the destroyed B-47 could be explained by the fact that, not one but two aircraft were destroyed. It should be pointed out that there has never been any official mention of a second plane being destroyed in this accident. I am including it purely as a possible explanation.

I recall being told an interesting story relating to this incident by a friend who lived in Newbury at the time. Apparently, he and other residents were given geiger counters to check the levels of radiation around their properties after the accident. These had to be replaced by more sensitive models because they failed to pick up any signs of significant radioactive contamination.

Map showing the locations of RAF Greenham Common and the Atomic Weapons Reasearch Establishment at Aldermaston in Berkshire. The former air base is 63 miles to the west of central London and is now a business park. It is 4 miles from Newbury and 6.5 miles from Aldermaston. This location is now known as The Atomic Weapons Establishment (A.W.E.) Aldermaston.

Bomb Dropped by Accident
Mars Bluff, South Carolina, US
11th March 1958

What happened to the Gregg family on that March afternoon in 1958 was truly the stuff of nightmares. One moment their home in the quiet community of Mars Bluff in South Carolina was a picture of domestic peace. The two daughters, six year old Helen and nine year old Frances were playing in the garden with their young cousin Ella. Meanwhile, their parents Greg and Effie were inside the house with their son Walter. The next moment everything was torn apart by a massive explosion leaving all six members of the Gregg family injured. Where the children's playhouse had been 200 yards away there was now a 70 foot wide crater.

The cause of this mayhem could be found 15,000 feet above them in the sky. The guilty party was a B-47 Stratojet carrying a consignment of Mk 6 H-bombs. As it overflew Mars Bluff from its base near Savannah, Georgia to RAF Bruntingthorpe in the UK, its Captain, Earl Koehler was alerted to a fault in the bomb bay. It seemed that there was a problem with the harness holding one of the nuclear bombs. He ordered the bombardier Captain Bruce Kulka down to investigate. Once in the bomb bay, Kulka reached around the bomb, but accidentally grabbed its release pin. He watched in horror as the deadly weapon smashed through the bomb bay doors and fell 15,000 feet to earth.

As it hit the playhouse on the Gregg's property, the high explosives within the bomb exploded leaving the huge crater and seven neighbouring buildings damaged. Fortunately, like all nuclear weapons aboard USAF planes, this bomb was not armed. For safety reasons the plutonium core for triggering the chain reaction was kept separate from its weapon until the plane neared its target. As a result, the explosion was conventional not nuclear.

Nevertheless, the fact that nobody on the ground was killed was a miracle in itself. Had the weather been poor, the Gregg girls and their cousin might well have been in the playhouse when the bomb hit killing them all. Alternatively, had the weapon fallen a few seconds earlier or later it might well have destroyed a group of houses leaving a death toll in double figures. The Greggs sued the U.S. Government and received damages of $54,000 - the equivalent of $478,526 in 2019.

Mars Bluff has gone down in history as the only town in the U.S. to be 'nuked' by its own side.

A Close Brush With Armageddon
B-52 crash
Goldsboro, North Carolina United States
24th January 1961

Like many small American towns, Eureka in North Carolina is not a place that the passing traveller would have cause to remember. However, there is one feature that sets it apart from all the other small towns in the United States. This is explained by an historical sign in the town with the following inscription :

'Nuclear Mishap
B-52 transporting 2 nuclear bombs crashed Jan 1961. Widespread disaster averted, 3 crewmen died 3 mi S.'

Behind this brief message lies a tragic story of a near brush with Armageddon. The dramatic events of what has become known as the Goldsboro B-52 crash began around about midnight on 24th January 1961.

High above the farmland of North Carolina, a B-52G Stratofortress carrying two Mark 39 thermonuclear bombs was commencing mid air refuelling from a tanker. Suddenly, the commander of the B-52, Major Walter Scott Tulloch, received an unwelcome message from the tanker: there was a fuel leak on the B-52's left wing.

The refuelling operation was immediately stopped and Tulloch informed ground control of the problem. He was ordered to fly out over the nearby coast to use up the bulk of the bomber's existing fuel load in a holding pattern.

By the time the B-52 arrived at the holding area, the leak had dramatically worsened with 37,000 pounds of fuel spilling out of it in 3 minutes. On reporting this, Tulloch was ordered to fly to Seymour Johnson Air Base near Goldsboro and make an emergency landing.

As the huge bomber lost height on its approach to the airbase, it became increasingly unmanageable. Finally, the crew lost control completely and the order was given to bail out at 9000 feet. Five crewmen either ejected or bailed out surviving their parachute landings. Another crew member ejected but was killed on landing. One of the three B-52 pilots Lt. Adam Mattocks managed to bail out of the top hatch of the B-52 becoming the only person ever to do so without an ejector seat and survive. Two other crew members died onboard.

The pilotless B-52 gyrated downwards, breaking up at about fifteen hundred feet and spilling its load of two 4 megaton nuclear bombs out of the plane. Aircraft wreckage and the nuclear weapons fell over two square miles of cotton and tobacco farmland around the small community of Faro.

When one of the two MK 39 thermonuclear bombs fell to earth something triggered the multitude of arming mechanisms on the bomb. Effectively, the bomb had been jolted into arming itself. Had the final arm/safe mechanism moved into the arm position, the weapon would have detonated with catastrophic results. Such an explosion in a bomb 250 times the size of the Hiroshima weapon would have wiped out a large part of the population of North Carolina and rendered the state uninhabitable for the foreseeable future.

Without its parachute opening, the bomb hit the ground in a tobacco field at 700 mph disintegrating and burying itself 20 feet deep in the sodden soil. Mercifully, the arm/safe switch did not engage before separating from the bulk of the bomb.

The other bomb's parachute did deploy causing the weapon to land in an upright position against a tree. It was discovered in this position with its parachute entangled in the tree's branches by the bomb disposal team led by Lt Jack ReVelle. On checking the intact weapon he located the arm/safe trigger which was in the safe position.

Whilst locating the wreckage of the second bomb buried in a tobacco field Lt ReVelle and his team made a truly frightening discovery. In an interview many years after the event, he described what actually happened:

"Until my death I will never forget hearing my sergeant say, 'Lieutenant, we found the arm/safe switch.' I said, "Great." He said, 'Not great. It's on arm.'"

Armageddon on mainland United States had been averted by the failure of just one arming switch.

That is not quite the end of the story. When trying to excavate the wreckage of the buried H-bomb, the Air Force team encountered insuperable problems with uncontrollable groundwater flooding. Eventually excavation of the bomb and its deadly cargo of highly radioactive uranium and plutonium was abandoned. It has remained in this doomsday grave beneath the tobacco fields of North Carolina ever since.

Mark 39 H-bomb where it came to rest against a tree after the Goldsboro crash in North Carolina.
Photo: USAF

Salvage team attempting to recover Mk39 H-bomb from a tobacco field at Faro near Goldsboro North Carolina. It is still there.
Photographs courtesy USAF

'Buzz One Four' B-52 crash
Savage Mountain, Maryland 13th January 1964

Chance, fate, Act of God or destiny, call it what you will, often intervenes to affect the course of our lives. This was certainly the case with the crew of a B-52 Stratofortress bomber which came to grief on a mountainside in the American state of Maryland in 1964. The plane's call sign of B14 would become well known as Buzz One Four.

On 13th January of that year, Captain Tom McCormick was ordered to travel from Turner Air Force Base at Albany in the state of Georgia to Westover AFB in Massachusetts to pick up B-52 Buzz One Four. This bomber had been part of the SAC operation known as *Chrome Dome* when it was diverted to Westover with mechanical problems. With the original crew now transferred, Tom McCormick was ordered to head up the relief crew to bring the now repaired Stratofortress back to its home base at Turner AFB.

The choice of this base for the back up crew to recover the Stratofortress was no accident since it was dedicated to SAC operations with each of its B-52s flying three to four *Chrome Dome* missions every month. Tom McCormick was very proud both of his job as a Captain of one of these Stratofortresses and his role in the *Chrome Dome* Defence operations. On this midwinter's day he bade farewell to his wife, no doubt reminding her, as he always did, that if anything happened he would phone her call/connect.

As with all the other crew members, the navigator Major Robert Payne found himself on this ferrying flight by chance. He had been ordered to phone around to find a navigator for the flight; when he drew a blank in this task, he volunteered himself for the job. Since it was quite a short flight, he also decided not to take his weatherproof night suit along. Both of these decisions would prove to have far reaching consequences for the father of three.

When the B-52 took off from Westover, Captain McCormick was ever mindful of his responsibility for not only the most expensive aircraft in the Air Force but also its cargo. This comprised two Mark 53 H-bombs whose combined power was 1100 times greater than the bomb dropped on Hiroshima.

He and the rest of the crew were also anxious about two storm fronts from the west and east that were destined to cross their path during the journey. As it happened, the plane found itself in the centre of this combined storm when they were over Maryland.

McCormick made repeated attempts to escape the worst of this raging storm by changing altitude. Then suddenly, the severe turbulence ripped the tailplane off rendering the huge bomber uncontrollable. As the B-52 turned upside down, Captain McCormick ordered the crew to bail out. Everyone managed to escape the aircraft except the bombardier Major Robert Townley who died in the crash. He left a widow and two young children.

Escaping the doomed bomber was not the end of the surviving crew's ordeal. They had parachuted into a fierce blizzard over mountainous terrain. The most fortunate was the Co-Pilot Captain Parker Peedin who landed in a forest with his survival kit intact. This enabled him to survive two nights in zero conditions before being the first survivor to be rescued.

The youngest crew member 27 year old Melvyn Wooten, the tail gunner had badly injured his leg on part of the aircraft as he bailed out. Weak with loss of blood and hampered by his injury he attempted to make it to the lights of a settlement close to where he landed. Sadly, he did not succeed and died of exposure. His body was not found for five days. His wife Carol had given birth to a daughter only a few days before.

Major Robert Payne, who had volunteered to be navigator found himself suspended thirty feet above the ground when his parachute became entangled in a lofty pine. He knew that if he stayed where he was, he would die of exposure, so he cut himself loose. Sadly, without his weatherproof suit and his survival kit with the parachute in the tree he died of exposure leaving a widow and three children.

Fourteen hours after the crash, Tom McCormick was spotted by a local farmer and his son struggling across a snow covered field close to exhaustion. They took him in to their house where Tom made two phone calls. One was to the Air Force authorities but the first was call/collect to his wife.

The B-52 had crashed on the side of Savage Mountain close to the little town of Grantsville in Maryland. Despite the terrible weather many of the locals turned out help in the search and rescue operation. One of them was a local stonemason who used his trucks to retrieve the two nuclear bombs.

The B-52 crashed on Savage Mountain because its tail, also known as vertical stabiliser, had been broken off by severe turbulence. This accident was by no means a one-off. Over the previous three years there had been four similar tail failure incidents involving B-52s that had cost the lives of 17 men. Only three days earlier a B-52 had lost its tail in similarly turbulent conditions over New Mexico. On that occasion, the pilot had actually managed to land the aircraft safely. As that particular B-52 was being used as a test bed to investigate structural failures at the time, the incident and safe landing were captured on film and photographs. It became the most famous of these incidents.

After the Savage Mountain crash it emerged that a year before a committee had been set up to examine the cause of these accidents. Its conclusion that the existing tail on the B-52 was too heavy to withstand stormy conditions proved to be the correct one. Sadly, fitting modified lighter tails to all B-52s was only enacted after the Savage Mountain crash. The reason why rectifying this well known problem was delayed is frankly a mystery.

The crash greatly affected the community at the small town of Grantsville. It was as if the town had lost some of its own sons in the disaster. Many of its residents helped pay for memorials to the three airmen who died as well as one commemorating the actual accident. The town has also regularly held days of commemoration since the tragedy.

In 2017 a documentary telling the full story of The Savage Mountain B-52 crash was released on Amazon Prime Video. Called *'Buzz One Four'* it has an especially personal angle on this tragedy. It was written, directed and narrated by Matt McCormick the grandson of Tom McCormick, the pilot of B-52 'Buzz One Four'.

B-52 Stratofortress similar to 'Buzz One Four" over Oxford, U.K.
Photograph by Nick Brazil

On January 10th 1964 this B-52H landed safely after losing its vertical stabiliser in stormy weather. It flew for five hours without its vertical stabiliser.
Photograph courtesy USAF/Boeing

B-52 Mid Air Collision, Palomares, Almeira, Andalusia, Spain 17th January 1966

On the mid morning of 17th January 1966, a B-52 Stratofortress of the Strategic Air Command was on the return leg of an SAC mission known as *Operation Chrome Dome*. This was an extremely long operation taking the aircraft from its USAF Base in North Carolina to the Soviet Border on the Black Sea. On board were four MK 28 H-bombs with a combined destructive capability four hundred times that of the A-bombs dropped on Hiroshima and Nagasaki. The distance of the mission was over 12,000 miles requiring two refuelling operations.

At approximately 10:30 a.m. the B-52 piloted by Major Larry G. Messinger, was at an altitude of 31,000 feet above the Mediterranean close to the little Spanish fishing village of Palomares. At this point a KC-135 tanker that had flown out of Morón Air Base in Spain was positioning itself just ahead of the B-52 to perform the second refuelling of the bomber's mission.

Air refuelling is a very delicate procedure that requires a high level of precision particularly from the refuelling boom operator in the tanker. If they think the receiving aircraft is getting little too close for comfort they will give the command: "Break away, Break away, Break away."

Even if all this is in place, accidents can still happen.

In the case of the SAC B-52 over Spain, Pilot Larry Messinger recalled they were approaching the KC-135 slightly too fast to the point where the B-52 started to overhaul the tanker. However, since there was no "Break away!" command from the KC-135 tanker Messinger assumed there was no danger of collision. He was wrong.

The next moment, the nozzle of the refuelling boom on the KC-135 collided with upper part of the B-52 fuselage. In the process, the left wing of the giant aircraft was torn off. This ignited the fuel in the B-52 and the KC-135 causing a huge explosion. The tanker was immediately enveloped in a massive fireball that killed all four of its crew members. Miraculously, five of the seven crew of the B-52 survived the initial explosion. As the huge plane began to plummet to earth, the crewmen bailed out. Only one did not survive. The navigator, Fl Lt Steven Montanus managed to eject but his parachute failed to open making him the third fatality of the B-52 crew.

As for the others, three, including Messinger landed in the sea and were rescued. A fourth, Captain Ivens Buchanan still trapped in his ejector seat but with his parachute open survived a hard landing inland.

Five miles off shore in the Mediterranean, local fisherman Francisco Simó Orts aboard the *Augustin y Rosa* fishing boat saw the two planes explode. A little later he watched as five parachutes floated down amidst a rain of debris landing in the sea. Crewmen on two of the parachutes appeared to be dead, one 'with his guts trailing'. In fact they were not dead crewmen at all but part of the parachute gear of the fourth H-bomb that had been aboard the B-52. A short while later, Orts rescued the pilot of the B-52, Larry Messinger from the drink. Three other crew members Orts had seen parachuting to the sea had also been rescued but the fourth and fifth could not be accounted for.

Presumably the bomb had sunk almost immediately it hit the surface. The other three bombs had all fallen inland close to Palomares village with one coming to rest on the bed of a stream. The impact had caused the conventional explosives within two of the bombs to explode scattering radioactive particles, including plutonium, over the village and surrounding farmland.

These explosives were part of the trigger used to cause the chain reaction in the nuclear weapon when it exploded. This process is relatively complex in order to avoid accidental detonation. As per standard practice, all four of the bombs aboard the B-52 were not armed with their plutonium triggers at the time.

This was just as well for if only one of the nuclear bombs landing near Palomares had actually detonated, the destruction in terms of life and property across a large part of Spain would have been unimaginable.

The village itself did not escape entirely unscathed. A large piece of plane wreckage landed in the local school playground whilst smaller bits from the aircraft rained down across the village. Miraculously, all the inhabitants survived unscathed.

Following the accident all United States bases in Spain were put on alert. 1,600 personnel ranging from cooks to musicians and military police were packed into buses to be taken to the Palomares area. The men were told it was part of a clean-up following a military aircraft crash. They were assured that there was absolutely no risk.

Once there, the servicemen fanned out across the farmland and tomato fields surrounding Palomares to pick up pieces of wreckage. What they did not know was that much of what they collected was contaminated with high levels of radiation including plutonium. None of these first responders to the accident were provided with any protective clothing. The USAF has always steadfastly maintained that there had never been any risk of radiation infecting these workers. However, over fifty years later many of the survivors are suffering from various cancers they are convinced were caused by the radiation from the Palomares crash.

The three bombs that fell on land were located within twenty four hours, whilst the fourth sank in the Mediterranean without trace. This was not only a fearful embarrassment for the U.S. military authorities but also a security headache. As long as it remained undiscovered there was always the danger that an unfriendly power such as the Soviets might recover the H-bomb before the Americans. The Spanish coastal population were also keen for this nuclear Sword of Damocles to be safely recovered. They feared that whilst the bomb lay on the seabed it could always explode or leak deadly amounts of radiation at some time in the future.

With only a vague idea where the bomb had landed, the USAF authorities were faced with the daunting task of searching a large area of the southern Mediterranean. On 22nd January, the Air Force contacted the United States Navy for help. They in turn convened a Technical Advisory Group to assess what vessels, equipment and personnel needed to be used in the search for the missing H-bomb.

One of the local people the U.S. military authorities also hired was Francisco Simó Orts the skipper of the trawler *Augustin E Rosa* who had actually seen the bomb hit the sea. Unsurprisingly, this gave Orts quite a bit of celebrity status in the local community where he earned the nickname *Paco el de la bomba* or *'Bomb Frankie'*.

With little to go on except the fisherman's verbal testimony as to where the bomb had landed, they employed a mathematical grid called The Bayesian Theory to search the area. This method of search has subsequently been successfully used on a number of occasions to locate vessels and aircraft lost at sea.

At the height of the search, the U.S. Navy had over twenty of their ships combing the area. In addition to this, there were a number of deep sea submersible vessels (DSV) and 150 qualified divers searching the Mediterranean depths. Nevertheless, it took them eighty days to locate the missing weapon. However, considering where it was, this is hardly a surprise. The bomb was at a depth of 2,550 feet on a steep slope of an uncharted subterranean canyon known as Rio Almanzora.

On 17th March 1966, DSV *Alvin* was sent down with a crew of three to bring the H-bomb back to the surface. *Alvin* is a remarkable deep submergence research vehicle capable of diving to a depth of 14,800 feet.

Taking her name from oceanographer Allyn Vine who was the vessel's main creator, she had been commissioned by the United States Navy in 1964.

This first attempt to recover the H-bomb failed with the weapon breaking loose as the recovery crew hauled it to the surface. The bomb then sank to the even greater depth of 2,990 feet.

On 7th April, *Alvin* located the H-bomb again at the greater depth. This time it was decided that a submersible better fitted to the task would be used to bring the bomb to the surface. The vehicle that was chosen was a Cable Controlled Undersea Recovery Vehicle (CURV-1).

Once again the mission seemed doomed to failure. Whilst a line was being attached to the bomb, the submersible became entangled with the weapon's parachute gear. However, the day was saved when it was decided to raise both the weapon and submersible in this tangled embrace. Finally the recovery team watched with relief as the H-bomb that had caused so much fear and anxiety and cost many millions of dollars to retrieve was lowered on to the deck of *USS Petrel*. The bomb was then transferred to another warship, *USS Cascade* which shipped it back to the United States.

That was by no means an end to the affair. When it came to the Palomares disaster there were quite a few parties with an axe to grind.

One of these was *'Bomb Frankie'*. Orts the fisherman who saw the H-bomb hit the sea and helped the U.S. military search for it. He reckoned the Government of the U S of A owed him big time! Without him that bomb would never have been found. So if they were not prepared to cough up he would have his day in court. That day came when Orts with his lawyer appeared in United States District Court for the Southern District of New York claiming salvage rights for the recovered H-bomb.

It seemed that under maritime law Orts had a pretty strong case. Which was no doubt why he could command the services of a very distinguished lawyer. In this case it was one Herbert Brownell former Attorney General under President Dwight Eisenhower. If the fisherman won his case against the U.S. Government, he was entitled to one per cent of the value of the H-bomb. Since that was valued by the U.S. Government at $2 billion, Orts would be in line for a payout of at least $20 million.

In the event, the U.S. Air Force settled out of court for an undisclosed sum that is thought to have been as low as $14,566. Orts remained dissatisfied complaining that the Air Force never lived up to their side of the financial agreement.

Then there were the local inhabitants of Palomares who, quite rightly, were seeking compensation for the damage and distress the accident had caused them and their livelihoods. In response, the United States Air Force settled 536 Spanish claims at a cost of $710,914.

General Franco's government then ruling Spain was also keen not to let what they saw as a valuable political opportunity go to waste. This was a time when relations between the Spanish Government and the U.K. were at an all time low because of the Franco Government's demands for the return of Gibraltar to Spanish sovereignty. Franco was exerting a great deal of pressure including the closure of the land border between Gibraltar and mainland Spain. In an official statement on 21st January, the Spanish Government said *'the Palomares incident was evidence of the dangers created by NATO's use of the Gibraltar airstrip'*. Following this announcement, the U.S. Government announced on 25th January that its planes would no longer overfly Spanish Territory with nuclear weapons. For good measure, the Spanish Government followed this up with an official ban of its own.

At the other end of the political spectrum, an underground communist group mounted a highly vocal protest outside the U.S. Embassy in Madrid. There had already been angry protests about the B-52 accident in the Palomares area. In an attempt to dampen down the growing firestorm, the American ambassador went for a highly publicised swim on the local beaches with the Spanish minister for tourism to show there was no danger of radiation.

Despite all this firefighting, the Palomares Incident began the process that would ultimately spell the end of the long distance SAC operations such as *Chrome Dome*.

In the meantime, the USAF clean-up around Palomares continued. A total of 5.4 acres of the most heavily contaminated soil was packed into 6,000 barrels and shipped back to a specialist nuclear location called The Savannah River Site in Georgia. Established in the 1950s primarily to process nuclear fuel and handle radioactive waste this 310 square mile site became the graveyard for Palomares' poisoned earth.

In spite of the extensive clean-up programme and removal of the irradiated soil, Palomares remains blighted by the accident. In 2004, nearly forty years after the event, some land around Palomares was found to be still heavily irradiated. This forced the Spanish Government to expropriate these poisoned areas. Like Banquo's ghost, the contamination from the Palomares Accident still keeps returning. In 2006 two trenches were discovered near the town cemetery containing a significant quantity of soil contaminated with plutonium.

However, the plutonium was considered not to be a threat provided it remained undisturbed. Whilst it is true that no detrimental health effects have been found amongst the local population since the crash, this is cold comfort to the local community. Many Palomares inhabitants feel the very fact this was where four H-bombs landed has cast a blight on the town. They point to Marbella not far down the coast which has prospered as a tourist centre whilst their own town has languished.

"Every time the story hits the media, it hurts tourism," local barman Andres Portillo told Gerry Hadden a journalist with Public Radio International. "A lot of people don't want to come here because they think the quality of life must be low, that cancer rates are higher when that's not the case at all."

In October 2015 it seemed that the problem of the remaining contaminated soil was near resolution. The then U.S. Secretary of State John Kerry and Spanish Foreign Secretary José Manuel García-Margallo drew up a 'statement of intent' that the two countries would draw up 'a binding agreement' to finally finish the Palomares clean up.

Unfortunately, at the time of writing in 2021, this agreement still does not appear to have materialised and the final clean up has yet to be started.

Sources

1) *BBC World Service, Public Radio International, and WGBH in Boston. The US Air Force lost 4 nuclear bombs in Spain 52 years ago — and the disaster is still being felt now*
Christopher Woody Business Insider Jan 17, 2018

H-bomb recovered from the Mediterranean at a depth of 2,990 feet on the deck of *USS Petrel* April 1966.

Photograph courtesy US Navy

Casings of two of the H-bombs dropped on the village of Palomares in 1966. They are now exhibited in the National Museum of Nuclear Science & History in Albuquerque, New Mexico.
Photograph by Marshall Astor of San Pedro USA via Wikipedia

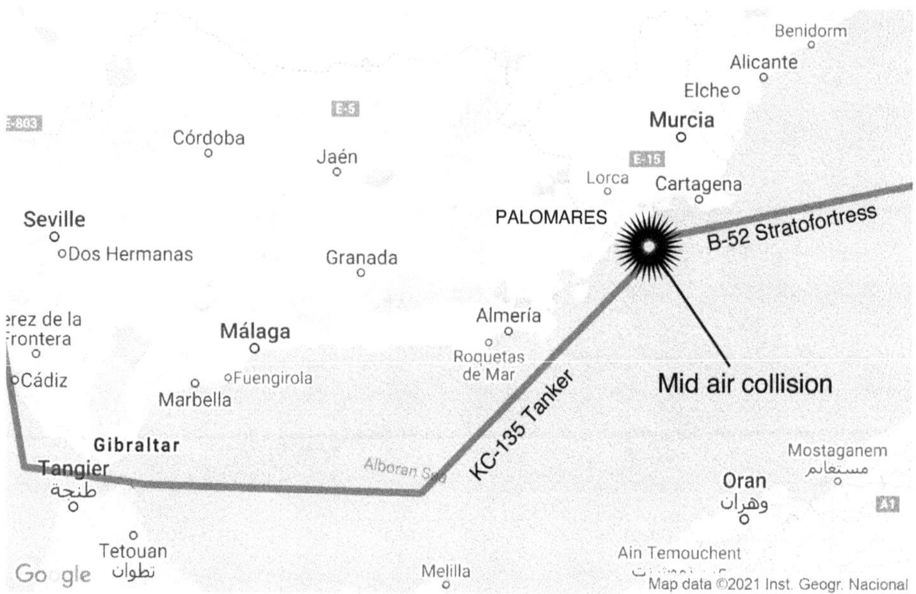

Map showing approximate route and site of collision between KC-135 Tanker and B-52 Stratofortress above fishing village of Palomares. Southern Spain 17th January 1966

Map created by Nick Brazil using Google Template

CURV-111 during the Pisces rescue.

US Navy Photograph

Footnote
Ahead of the CURV

The Cable Controlled Underwater Recovery Vehicle (CURV) that finally recovered the missing H-Bomb in the B-52 Palomares Accident, was developed by a branch of the United States Navy in the 1960s.

At the time, The Naval Ordnance Test Station were tasked to come up with a submersible that could recover weaponry that had been lost at great depths. CURV-1 was their answer and it was one that would distinguish itself over the years.

Originally it was developed to recover ordnance from a depth of 2,000 feet from the sea near the Navy's live firing range at San Clemente Island off the Californian coast. Its successor CURV-III became famous for successfully recovering the lost H-Bomb from the sea off Palomares in Spain in 1966. In this, CURV-III succeeded where the miniature submersible *Alvin* had failed, lifting the bomb from a depth of nearly 3,000 feet.

In 1973, CURV-III was literally a lifesaver when it recovered *Pisces III* a submersible that had sunk off the coast of Ireland. *Pisces* was laying transatlantic telecommunications cable at the time when her buoyancy tank accidentally flooded causing her to sink to the seabed at a depth of 1,575 feet (480 metres).

After seventy-six nail biting hours, the two man crew of *Pisces* were rescued with only minutes to spare before their oxygen ran out. It goes down in history as the deepest undersea rescue of all time.

Sources

Chapman, Roger (1975). *No Time On Our Side.* W.W. Norton & Co., New York ISBN 0-393-03186-1

Pisces III: A dramatic underwater rescue. Vanessa Barford BBC News Magazine 30th August 2013

A Fire On The Ice
B-52 Crash, Thule Air Base, Greenland
21st January 1968

It is remarkable how sometimes a small error can lead to a major catastrophe. This was certainly the case in January 1968 when B-52 bomber serial number 58-0188 took off from Plattsburgh Air Force Base, New York. As part of SAC's *Chrome Dome* Operation, this Stratofortress was assigned to travel out over Baffin Bay in Canada. The route of this operation would take the bomber over Thule BMEW (Ballistic Missile Early Warning System) Air Base in Greenland. An important part of this mission was to monitor the Base's communications system to ensure it was functioning correctly. The aircraft's payload included four B28FI thermonuclear bombs.

Before take off, one of the six crew performed a seemingly innocuous action that would prove to have drastic consequences a few hours later. One of the pilots, a Major Alfred D'Mario, placed three cloth covered foam cushions over the heating vent under the instructor navigator's seat. Shortly after take off another cushion was added to the three.

The flight was uneventful until the aircraft was ninety miles from Thule. At that point D'Mario opened up the engine bleed valve to draw in extra warm air to heat up the uncomfortably cold cabin. As the hot air from the engines travelled through the cabin's heating ducts it ignited the cushions. Smelling burning, the navigator searched for the fire. By the time he discovered its source the blaze was well under way. Despite using two fire extinguishers, he was unable to put out the fire which then spread to the rest of the cabin.

The other crew members also fought the blaze but in spite of exhausting a further five extinguishers they were unable to damp down the flames. With the cabin rapidly filling with thick smoke, the crew were unable to see their instruments to perform an emergency landing at nearby Thule Air Base. The Captain was left with no option but order the evacuation of the B-52. All seven crew members bailed out of the aircraft with the co-pilot Leonard Svitenko sustaining fatal head injuries in the process.

The now pilotless B-52 flew on for another seven miles beyond the air base. It then turned 180 degrees and glided down to hit the sea ice at an angle of 20 degrees. The impact ignited the conventional explosives in the four nuclear bombs on board spreading radioactive particles over a wide area. This explosion also caused the aircraft's 225,000 pounds of fuel to ignite. The subsequent conflagration melted the sea ice sending both the bomber and its deadly cargo to the sea bed.

Because of the extreme conditions of the arctic winter, the only search and rescue teams comprised sledge teams of local Inuit. Under the guidance of Jens Zinglerson, the local representative of The Royal Greenland Trade Department, they rescued all the surviving crew of the aircraft. Zinglerson would receive the Air Force Exceptional Civilian Service Medal from the U.S. Ambassador, K. E. White for his role in this heroic endeavour.

Immediately after the accident, the American and Danish authorities launched *Project Crested Ice* to clean up the crash site. Despite the extreme conditions of the arctic winter there was considerable pressure to complete this as quickly as possible and for good reason.

Firstly, there was an extensive area of blackened surface ice where the aircraft had impacted. This was heavily contaminated with aircraft fuel and radioactive particles including plutonium. It was feared that if this was not cleared before the spring, the contaminated ice would melt into the ocean causing widespread pollution. Secondly, there was the thorny job of retrieving the plane wreckage and four H-bombs from the ocean floor.

By the time *'Operation Freezelove'* (as some wag dubbed it) was completed nine months after the accident, 550,000 gallons of contaminated liquid had been removed from the site and shipped to the U.S. The total cost of the clean-up is estimated to have been $69 million by 2020 values. Much of this operation had been conducted in the pitch dark of the Arctic winter in average temperatures of -40 degrees F (-40 C).

At the insistence of the Danish Authorities, all the blackened and contaminated ice was removed from the crash area. This demand was hardly surprising since some of the radioactive particles at the crash site, such as uranium 234 and uranium 235, had half lives of 250,000 years and 700 million years. It was estimated by the man in charge of this operation, General Hunziker, that 93% of the radioactive material was shipped back to the United States.

Part of this clean-up operation involved a difficult undersea search for some or all of the missing H-bombs. As in the Palomares incident in Spain, a mini submarine was used. It remains unclear how successful this search was and whether the fourth bomb was ever recovered. It is also unclear how much the U.S. authorities told their Danish counterparts.

Over the years controversy has continued to surround the Thule crash and its clean-up. From time to time, allegations that the U.S. military were only able to recover three of the four nuclear weapons have surfaced in the Danish and international press. The Pentagon has always maintained that all four nuclear weapons were destroyed in the crash. (1)

In 2008, a BBC report based on research of 348 declassified documents appeared to establish that the Americans had actually lost one of their H-bombs. This was subsequently contradicted by the Danish Government who commissioned their own study of the documents by The Danish Institute of International Studies. So, not for the first or last time in the history of such cases the jury remains out.

With or without the missing bomb, the Thule crash was sufficiently serious to lead to the subsequent suspension of any further *Chrome Dome* flights. This was partly due to a genuine fear that if the B-52 had come down on the Thule early warning array instead of the ice if could well have been mistaken for a first strike attack triggering World War Three. In 1971 the U.S. and Soviet Governments agreed to notify each other in the case of crashes involving nuclear weapons such as the Thule or Palomares incidents.

The Thule accident had also heightened concern in the U.S. military and government circles about the way high explosives within nuclear weapons tended to ignite on impact. This spurred the authorities to find a safer alternative. In 1979, after research and experimentation at the Los Alamos Laboratories, a less volatile explosive known as Insensitive High Explosive was found for nuclear weapons.

The long term ramifications of the Thule crash continued to return to haunt both the American and Danish governments for many years afterwards. As far back as 1957, at the time of the Paris NATO Summit, the Danish Government had a policy not to allow stockpiling of nuclear weapons on any part of its sovereign territory. This included The Thule Base that had been in American hands since the end of the Second World War.

In 1993, United States Government documents relating to the Thule Base and the B-52 crash were declassified. They revealed that, contrary to assertions by the Danish Government, USAF nuclear armed bombers were regularly overflying Greenland. Since it was Danish territory this was considered a breach of Denmark's non-nuclear policy. The documents also revealed that the B-52 bomber which crashed at Thule in 1968 was not attempting a one-off emergency landing as previously stated by the Danish and U.S. Governments. In fact it was on a regular mission overflying Greenland.

This ignited a huge political scandal in Denmark that became known as *'Thulegate'*. Pressured and embarrassed by these revelations, the Danish Government commissioned an enquiry by The Danish Institute of International Affairs into the whole question of whether or not the U.S. had violated Denmark's non-nuclear policy.

Their extensive report which was presented to Parliament in January 1997 confirmed that although the United States had been regularly overflying Greenland with nuclear armed bombers this had not breached any agreement with Denmark. For this, they blamed H.C. Hansen, the Danish Prime Minister at the time of the original agreement. Apparently, the matter of Denmark's non-nuclear policy was never mentioned in the meetings regarding the status of the Thule Base between Hansen and the U.S. Ambassador. This omission provided a loophole for the U.S. to make nuclear overflights without technically breaking the compact between the two countries.

The Institute's report provided yet more embarrassment for the Danish Government. Prior to its release, Niels Helveg Petersen, the Danish Foreign Minister had insisted that nuclear overflights notwithstanding, no U.S. nuclear weapons had been stockpiled on Danish Territory. However, the D.I.I.A. report subsequently revealed that between 1958 and 1968 at least seventy nuclear weapons were stored at the Thule Base **(2)**.

The report held another shock for Danish politicians and public when it revealed details of a top secret U.S. plan called *Iceworm*. Initiated in 1960, *Project Iceworm* was a U.S. military programme to install a 4,000 kilometre (2,500 mile) network of mobile launch sites under the Greenland ice cap. In the event of a war breaking out between the Soviet Union and the United States, they would be used to launch nuclear armed missiles on Russian cities and militarily strategic sites.

Iceworm was so secret that the US Government did not inform the Danish Government about it. Instead, the U.S. Department of Defense gave the scheme a public face called *Camp Century*. This project, they told the Danish Government, was to test the viability of small military outposts powered by mobile nuclear reactors. One of the purposes of such camps was to conduct scientific experiments on the ice cap.

The initial test camp was constructed 150 miles North of Thule and was a quite formidable project. Consisting of 3,000 metres of tunnels, it housed a shop, hospital, theatre and a church. Power came from the world's first mobile nuclear power station (*See SL-1 Reactor disaster Chapter 9*). The instability of the ice caused by the constant movement of the glacier rendered the project unworkable and it was abandoned in 1967.

Unfortunately, *Camp Century* was in such a remote location it was assumed it would be buried forever beneath the ice. So, no clean-up or removal operation was carried out. With the constant movement of the ice and possible glacial shrinkage, this certainly can not be taken for granted. If, as predicted by some scientists, what remains of the complex is exposed to the atmosphere, there could be severe ecological implications. Contaminants from within the base include 200,000 litres of diesel fuel, radioactive particles and PCBs (toxic organic chlorine compound).

Although it happened over fifty years ago, many uncomfortable and unanswered questions about the Thule crash remain. Not least is that of the health of the Danish workers involved in *Operation Crested Ice* as the clean-up operation was known. None of them were given special protective clothing or were monitored for health problems by the US authorities.

In 1986, the then Danish Prime Minister Poul Schlüter commissioned a health survey of the former Thule workers by the Danish Institute for Clinical Epidemiology. After an eleven month investigation it concluded that the prevalence of cancer amongst this group was forty per cent higher than the general population. Another body, The Danish Institute of Cancer Epidemiology, found the abnormal cancer rates amongst these workers to be even higher at 50%. However, in spite of this neither body could definitely conclude this was down to radiation from the clean-up.

In 1987 two hundred of these workers took the U.S. Government to court to claim damages due to radiation. Although the action was unsuccessful it unlocked a mountain of classified documents that proved to be very revealing. One of the most damning facts to emerge was that the U.S. workers involved in the clean-up had not been regularly monitored for health problems. In 1995 a survey of 1,500 workers found that 450 (about a third) had died of cancer. In that same year the Danish Government paid 1,700 of the former *Crested Ice* workers compensation of 50,000 krone each (£5,700 in 1995 values).

However, the Danish Government does not accept that radiation from the Thule Accident has adversely affected the health of either the workers or residents around the base. In 2011, a report by the Danish National Board of Health stated that *'the total radiation dose for*

National Board of Health stated that *'the total radiation dose for representative persons in the Thule area for plutonium contamination resulting from the 1968 Thule accident is lower than the recommended reference level, even under extreme conditions and situations.'*

As in so many cases of nuclear incidents dealt with in this book, the Thule Accident illustrates the difficulty in proving whether long term health problems are definitely linked to its radioactive contamination.

There is also the question of whether the B-52 crash did any long term damage to the environment. To assess this, the area has been scientifically monitored on a regular basis since the crash. A substantial part of this monitoring were eight scientific expeditions to the area for that purpose between 1968 and 2003. The conclusion of the 1997 expedition was that there was some residual radioactive contamination of the marine environment. Most of this was in the form of uranium 235 and plutonium. The amount was sufficiently small to present a minimal risk to human health.

Map showing location of Thule Base in Greenland

1) In view of the fact that a large amount of the conventional explosives in the nuclear bombs exploded on impact, this could well be correct.

2) *DIIS - The Danish Institute for International Studies* is a public institute for independent research and analysis of international affairs, financed by the Danish Government.

The Thule Crash - Joseph Thomas' Story

"I was a still photographer in Thule Air Force Base, Greenland when a B-52 crashed near the base. I was called to go out - I grabbed a 4x5 Speed Graphic - with a rescue team to search for survivors. We found and rescued the tail gunner and I got one shot. The photo was released to the media worldwide. "

Joseph Thomas' picture of the B-52. gunner (centre), SSgt Calvin Snapp, being rescued after ejecting onto the ice.

This photograph by Joseph Thomas shows some of the inuit who were employed at Thule. Local inuit teams played an important role in the rescue of the crew from the crashed B-52.

"The Air Force hired the inuit and their dog teams to go to and from the site because the ice on the bay was too thin to bear the weight of heavy motorised vehicles."

Chapter 9
SL - 1 Mobile Reactor Accident
National Reactor Testing Station, Idaho Falls, 3rd January 1961

At the height of the Cold War in the mid 1950s, the United States Government established a line of early warning radar stations in the Canadian Arctic. Known as the Defence Early Warning or DEW Line, they were the first line of defence against Soviet attack. In addition to the Canadian stations, there were also similar radar stations in the Aleutian Islands, Iceland, the Faroe Islands and Greenland (See '*A Fire On The Ice*' page 114).

One of the many logistical problems of having such complex establishments in remote and inhospitable places was providing reliable power and heat. This not only required the costly construction of boilers and diesel generators but also the ability to fly in a regular supply of fuel to run them and provide maintenance crews on 24 hour standby.

With this in mind, a specialist unit of the U.S. Armed Forces began researching a nuclear alternative to this problem. The name of this division was The Army Reactor Unit. Their idea was to develop portable nuclear power stations to provide heat and energy to the DEW Radar Stations on a 24/7 basis. Such power units would do away with the need for large on site fuel storage tanks, risky refuelling operations in poor weather conditions and generators running twenty-four hours a day.

Between 1954-55, the Army Reactor Unit of the United States Armed Forces began working on a prototype portable reactor with The Argonne National Laboratory (ANL) which is operated by The University of Chicago. ANL was established in 1946 as part of The *Manhattan Project* to assist Enrico Fermi in his work on nuclear reactors.

The main requirements for the portable reactor were very straightforward; all components had to be suitable for air transportation, they had to be standard to allow easy on site construction of the reactor which also had to be as simple and reliable as possible. The reactor had to be resistant to the extremes of Arctic weather conditions. One nuclear fuel core had to run the reactor for three years.

The prototype was the Argonne Stationary Low Power Reactor Number One (SL -1) built at The National Reactor Testing Station at Idaho

Falls in the summer of 1957. This was a boiling water reactor using highly enriched uranium fuel. It was housed in a cylindrical steel tower 48 feet high and 38.5 feet in diameter. After an intensive test period, it was handed over to the U.S. Army for training and operational experience in December 1958.

On 3rd January 1961, the reactor was being prepared for restart after an eleven day shutdown over Christmas and New Year. This task was entrusted to three army specialists John Byrnes, Richard Leroy McKinley and construction electrician Richard Legg.

Restarting the reactor was a very delicate operation requiring the central control rod to be gently and manually removed a distance of just four inches. This time, something went terribly wrong. The rod was removed 26 inches - far too far and fast. Instantly, this caused a violent explosion known as a criticality accident which started an uncontrolled chain reaction.

Within a matter of seconds, the fuel in the reactor core melted and vaporised sending a mass of water hurtling to the roof of the reactor building at 159 feet per second. The pressure of this "water hammer" was such that the reactor structure was propelled nine feet upwards to hit the chamber roof before falling back down to the ground. The explosion filled the whole building with a mixture of highly radioactive steam and wreckage.

Whilst all three men sustained fatal injuries in the blast, the level of radiation they were subjected to was also unsurvivable.

Because the three men involved in this terrible accident are all dead, the reason why the control rod was wrongly extracted will never be known. After a two year investigation, four theories were posited for this:

- Sabotage or suicide
- Suicide-murder
- Operator error
- An attempt to make the control rod come out more smoothly. Apparently 'sticky' control rods were not a totally rare occurrence.

  The first two theories indicate that investigators had strong reasons to believe there was some sort of friction between at least two of the three operatives.

As a result of the accident, the design of portable reactors was completely changed. To prevent similar criticality accidents occurring, future designs did not allow the central control rod to be removed or manipulated manually.

The operation to clean up and dispose of what was left of the SL-1 reactor and its buildings took eighteen months and involved 475 people. Most of the debris from the accident was buried close to the original site of the SL-1 reactor within the NRTS site.

Whilst the increasing costs of the Vietnam War forced the U.S. Military to curtail the Mobile Reactor Programme in 1965, a small number of these reactors continued to be used until 1975.

The SL-1 Tragedy was the first peacetime nuclear accident in history.

SL - 1 Mobile Reactor at the National Reactor Testing Station, Idaho Falls prior to the accident.

Photograph: Argonne Laboratory/US Government

Scientist checking Highway 20 near to the site of the SL-1 accident for radiation shortly after the incident.
Photograph: INEEL/US Government

Burial site of the radioactive remains of the SL-1 Reactor in the grounds of the NRTS Idaho Falls.
Photograph: US Environmental Ptection Agency

Chapter10
The French Nuclear Legacy
1962 to 1996

By 1962 The French Government had abandoned the atmospheric testing of her nuclear weapons in favour of underground explosions. The site she chose for these subterranean tests was at In Eker a small village in the Sahara about 150 kilometres north of the oasis city of Tamanrasset. At that time, this was still part of France, but would become part of the independent state of Algeria within months.

The underground test of a hydrogen bomb under the codename Béryl was scheduled for May1st 1962. It is unlikely that such a significant date as May Day was a coincidence. Indeed, many officials had been invited to observe the test. The most important of these were French Defence Minister Pierre Messmer and Gaston Palewski, a close confidant of President Charles De Gaulle.

The bomb was detonated in an underground shaft situated in a nearby mountain area called Tan Afella. Unfortunately, the heavy doors of the shaft had been improperly sealed. Eyewitnesses report seeing a huge flame similar to a giant blow torch shoot upwards from the ground. This was rapidly followed by a reddish brown cloud that turned black as it rose 9000 feet (2,600 metres) in the air.

A significant quantity of radioactive particles also escaped from the shaft and drifted 150 kilometres downwind from the site. It also drifted over the command and observation point irradiating many of the observers including Messmer and Palewski. After decontamination, the two men hurriedly left for Paris on the same day.

Nine soldiers of the 621st Groupe d'Armes Spéciales received very high doses of radiation from the cloud as they travelled from an outlying observation post to the command centre. At the time of writing, nearly sixty years after the event, it has not been possible to discover the precise numbers of injuries or fatalities (if any) that resulted from this accident. Pierre Messmer did die of cancer in 2007 at the advanced age of 91. Palewski succumbed to leukaemia in 1983. Whether these terminal illnesses could be linked to an incident that occurred many years before is anybody's guess.

Until recently, the numbers of the local Saharan population affected by that cloud of radioactivity was unknown. No records were kept of the number of deaths or health problems that occurred as a result of radiation poisoning from this accident. However, in 2010 secret military documents came to light detailing some of the damage done to both the environment and populations by the Saharan and Polynesian nuclear tests. As a result the French Government has now acknowledged that both their Saharan and Polynesian nuclear tests had damaged both local populations and the environments.

In 2010, a French pressure group for French military veterans *Armament Watchdog* released confidential military documents detailing the use of French troops as guinea pigs in that country's Saharan nuclear tests. These formerly secret documents detail how French troops were ordered to take part in military exercises within 700 yards of the blast zone. The soldiers concerned wore only minimal protective gear such as conventional gas masks The alleged purpose of exposing the troops in this way was to study the physical and mental effects of nuclear blasts on humans

According to the group's co founder, Patrick Bouveret: 'They deliberately sent people to do manoeuvres to test their reactions in the face of a nuclear explosion. Until now, we had a few witness accounts of manoeuvres involving armoured vehicles, not people...It's scandalous.'

'We were the atom guinea pigs,' said Guy Peyrachon, a veteran who had taken part in such exercises 10 kilometres from a nuclear blast. He was dressed only in shorts at the time. When he was twenty-five, he developed thyroid cancer and has suffered from bouts of epilepsy in the years since the tests. His thirty- year old son also has thyroid cancer.

Lucien Parfait, another veteran of the tests has lost his nose due to cancer that he blames on the nuclear blasts.

In January 2010, French legislators passed a law allowing victims of the country's nuclear tests to claim compensation for illnesses related to these nuclear explosions. It was not just the military who suffered from the effects of all the French nuclear tests. Algerian nuclear physics professor, Abdul Kadhim al Aboudi has done extensive research into the effects of the French tests on the local population.

His estimate is that 60,000 people were living within the area of the tests and therefore could have been irradiated. Other estimates put the number of Algerians who died as a result of irradiation from the tests as high as 42,000. Unfortunately, these are only estimates based on surveys conducted many years after the tests. So, it is difficult, if not impossible to verify these results. However, it can be safely assumed that large numbers of the local population either died or were made ill as a result of the tests.

The inhabitants of the Southern Sahara are not the only people due compensation for the effects of French nuclear tests. For thirty years between 1966 and 1996, the French military conducted a total of 193 nuclear tests in the islands of Muraroa and Fangataufa in her Polynesian territories.

However, in March 2021, the investigative website *Disclose* released details of over 2000 military documents which it had obtained under Freedom of Information legislation. They revealed that the French military covered up the extent to which the islands of French Polynesia had been irradiated by the nuclear tests. It estimated that the entire population of French Polynesia had been affected by the radiation from the blasts.

The health effects of all this can be seen in the enhanced numbers of cancer cases in the area. For example cases of thyroid cancer in the 280,000 population of the region are 30% higher than in metropolitan France. To date, Civen, an official compensation board has paid out compensation to 454 members of the military and civilians. This includes just 63 inhabitants of French Polynesia. This is a fraction of the people affected. 80 per cent of the claims that have come before Civen have been rejected without reasons given.

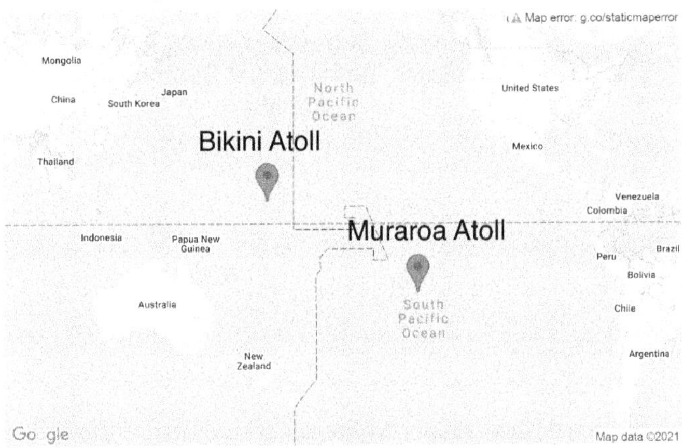

Map showing the U.S.Nuclear Pacific testing ground at Bikini Atoll and the French Pacific Nuclear testing site at Muraroa Atoll in French Polynesia.

Two maps showing location of French nuclear tests in the Sahara Desert.
Maps created by Nick Brazil using Google Template

Chapter 11
The Dounreay Shaft Explosion
Dounreay, Caithness, Scotland
10th May 1977

Situated nine miles west of the town of Thurso on the hauntingly beautiful northern Scottish coast, Dounreay is a place with a long history. Its name is Gaelic for 'fort on a mound' and the remains of an ancient castle still exist there.

In 1437, it was the site of the fierce Battle of Sandside Chase in which the Macdonald Clan slaughtered the local Caithness clansmen. During the Second World War it became an airfield known as RAF Station Dounreay and then *HMS Tern* after it was handed over to the Admiralty by RAF Coastal Command in 1944.

In the early 1950s, the now redundant airfield was taken over by the newly established United Kingdom Atomic Energy Authority (UKAEA). This isolated spot on the wild Caithness coast was ideal for their purposes to develop fast breeder nuclear reactor technology. Should an accident such as an explosion occur, the site was well away from any major town or city to cause a significant number of deaths or casualties. As a further safety precaution, the first reactor was encased in a one hundred and thirty-nine foot steel sphere.

By 1955, the Dounreay Nuclear Power Development Establishment, as the site was now known, had five reactors. Three of these were operated by the UKAEA and the other two by the Ministry of Defence.

On the civilian side, the main purpose of the Dounreay reactors was to develop the UK's fast breeder reactor technology. Two of the civilian reactors were fast breeder reactors whilst the third was a thermal research reactor to test materials used in the research programme.

The two other reactors operated by the MoD were on a separate site within the Dounreay complex known as The Vulcan Naval Reactor Test Establishment (NRTE). Their main purpose was to develop and test nuclear power plants for the Royal Navy's fleet of nuclear submarines.

Over the following forty years until its closure in 1994, Dounreay became a major local employer which greatly helped the growth and prosperity of nearby Thurso. The subsequent decommissioning and clean up of the site will still require a significant workforce until completion in 2025.

During the whole of its working life, none of the actual reactors on either the UKAEA or MoD sites posed any safety problems. However, in May 1977, the plant experienced a frightening reminder of the need to be ever vigilant when dealing with nuclear technology.

This wake up call centred on a two hundred foot shaft that had been drilled into the rock close to the coastline and some way from the reactors in 1959. Its original purpose was to allow low level nuclear waste to be dumped into the sea. In reality it became a waste dump for all manner of high and low level radioactive waste.

As more and more radioactive materials were dumped down the shaft, coastal erosion led to an inflow of both seawater and groundwater. On 10th May 1977, sodium and potassium waste that had been dumped into the shaft reacted with water flooding in from the sea and surrounding aquifer. This caused a violent hydrogen gas explosion.

The concrete lid at the top entrance of the shaft was blown off and scaffolding poles and debris were scattered as far as thirty feet away. A plume of white smoke was seen blowing across the sea. More seriously, highly radioactive particles including uranium, aluminium, caesium and plutonium were scattered over the surrounding countryside. This included two beaches, where highly radioactive particles continue to be found forty years later. At least one beach near to the plant has been closed to the public since 1983.

The explosion was not the only radiation leakage problem experienced at Dounreay. The shaft itself should have been properly sealed off from the sea. However, it proved to be highly porous allowing radioactive particles to leak out onto the neighbouring seabed. The currents also carried other radioactive particles to be deposited further down the coast.

In addition to this, over the next thirty years countless radioactive particles are thought to have escaped from the plant with water draining from the reactor's cooling ponds. These particles have been detected in the sea and on the beaches surrounding Dounreay.

Whilst these radioactive particles are very small, usually about the size of a grain of sand, they are also very deadly and have a long life. In the case of plutonium, the most dangerous, this is up to 24,000 years.

In fact, what happened at Dounreay has proved to be a textbook example of how not to dispose of nuclear waste.

Partly due its remote location, but also possibly because of the secrecy surrounding Dounreay's operations, little was known about these radioactive leakages until the 1990s and 2000s. In 1995, Rob Edwards wrote a detailed article about the radiation leaks for *The New Scientist.* Titled *"Lid Blown off Dounreay's Lethal Secret"* he described the shaft explosion in detail as well as the other radiation leaks that had occurred over a thirty year period. **(1)**

He also revealed that in 1987, The Committee on the Medical Aspects of Radiation in the Environment (COMARE) had asked the UKAEA to list all 'unplanned discharges' from the plant. This request was sparked by COMARE's investigation into a cluster of childhood leukaemia cases in the Dounreay area.

We should also spare a thought for Geoffrey Minter who bought the Reay Estate close to Dounreay in 1990. This included the beautiful Sandside Beach.

'When I came here, I thought I'd realised a dream,' he told journalist Simon Barber for an article in the *Daily Telegraph* in 2006. **(2)**

'There's a beautiful golf course looking out over the bay, and some excellent wild salmon fishing. Nobody knew about contamination then."

In 1997, his dream was shattered when Sandside Bay was fenced off after inspectors from Dounreay had found a radioactive particle on the beach. Although they assured the landowner this was a one-off event further radioactive particles have been discovered in subsequent years.

It is fair to say that the ramifications of the shaft explosion and radiation leaks have been considerable. However, care must be taken not to automatically conclude that all environmental and health problems are down to the radioactive discharges at Dounreay.

For example, the increase in instances of childhood leukaemia in the surrounding area is thought by some to stem from the explosion and leak at the shaft. However, in a paper by Sarah C Derby and Richard Doll published in the *British Medical Journal* in 1987 they concluded that *'the available data weigh heavily against the hypothesis that the recent increase in childhood leukaemia near Dounreay might be accounted for by exposure to radiation due to discharges from Dounreay and Sellafield.'*

So what is the state of play with Dounreay now? The shaft has not been used for disposal of waste since the explosion in 1977. In April 2019, it was announced that a massive clear-up of the site involving the award of six contracts to 30 companies would begin in the following year. This includes the retrieval of the waste from the offending shaft. It will be demolished along with the laboratories and contaminated water silo. It is estimated that it will be three hundred years before unrestricted use of the site will be possible.

In September 2020, the British Government announced that a £7.5 million contract *"For the world's deepest nuclear clean-up"* had been awarded to Nuvia, an international company specialising in nuclear engineering and management. Its partner in this will be Graham Construction. Work on cleaning the nuclear waste from the 65 metre shaft began in the autumn of 2020.**(3)**

Sadly the contamination of the surrounding beaches and seabed by radioactive particles seems likely to be a permanent legacy of Dounreay's history of lax waste disposal.

In September 2011,The Scottish Environmental Protection Agency announced its original plan to return the seabed to 'pristine condition' was simply not feasible. Although a total of 2,300 radioactive particles were removed from the neighbouring seabed between 2008 and 2011 others remain. It is possible but unlikely that amongst these are fragments of caesium-137 which has a half life of 30 years and plutonium-239 with a half life of 24,000 years. The latter is so deadly that the tiniest grain is lethal if ingested and can develop into cancer many years later. Fishing has also been banned within a two kilometre radius of the Dounreay Plant. Also, beaches that were formerly popular tourist spots are now considered unsafe.

Whilst they are on a much smaller scale, the Dounreay contamination accidents have eerie echoes of the Kyshtym/Mayak Disasters in the 1950s and 1960s. In both cases, lax disposal protocols have had far reaching consequences. Whether in Russia, Scotland or wherever, the lesson remains the same: you can never be too careful when dealing with nuclear energy and its radioactive waste.

Sources

1). *Rob Edwards, New Scientist 1995*

2). *Simon Barber for an article in the Daily Telegraph* in 2006.

3) *"Contract for world's deepest nuclear clean-up awarded"* HMG 9/09/20

Dounreay Nuclear Power Development Establishment, Nr Thurso, Caithness, Northern Scotland
Photograph by Terry Kettlewell/Shutterstock

Map showing location of Dounreay Nuclear Power Development Establishment, Nr Thurso, Caithness, Northern Scotland
Map by Nick Brazil using Google template

Chapter 12
Almost a China Burn
The Three Mile Island Reactor Partial Meltdown
Harrisburg, Pennsylvania, U.S.
March 28th 1979

Sometimes, the most far reaching events have very small, even innocent beginnings. In the case of the Three Mile Island nuclear accident in Pennsylvania it all began with a simple blockage.

Construction on The Three Mile Island nuclear power plant was commenced in 1974 at a site near the town of Londonderry Township in Pennsylvania. It is called Three Mile Island because of its location on a small island three miles downstream from the Borough of Middletown on the Susquehanna River. At the time of construction, the plant consisted of two pressurised water reactor (PWR) units known as TMI-1 and TMI-2. The second of these reactors was completed in 1978.

Like all nuclear power plants, the purpose of Three Mile Island is to generate electricity for the public grid. It does this by creating steam to drive the generators that produce the electricity. That steam is created by the heat from the nuclear reaction that occurs within the core of the plant's reactor. This process is also known as fission.

The Three Mile Island nuclear reactor is fuelled by containers of enriched uranium (fuel elements) that are inserted into the reactor. The uranium atoms are split within the reactor creating a high level of heat. The insertion or removal of cadmium rods into the reactor impedes the neutrons that are the subatomic particles that help drive the fission process. In this way, the cadmium rods control the speed of this nuclear reaction and if necessary, bring it to a halt.

The reactor and its uranium fuel are immersed in water that is in a closed loop because it is highly radioactive. The purpose of this water is twofold: 1) As the heat transfer to create the steam to drive the electricity generators. 2) To cool and control the temperature within the nuclear reactor. During the fission process, this water reaches a temperature of 600 degrees Fahrenheit. To prevent boiling, the water is pressurised.

The reactor is housed in a shell of eight inch thick steel within a building of concrete not less than 1.4 metres thick. This serves to contain any radioactivity in the case of an accidental leak and protection from external attack by terrorists for example.

Also within the reactor building is a steam generator or heat exchanger. This generator is divided into two parts. The first part contains the water to be heated into steam. This water is drawn from an external source such as a river or the sea. In the case of Three Mile Island, the source was the Susquehanna River.

The heated water from the reactor is pumped into the second part of the steam generator and through a series of metal tubes that extend into the section containing the external water. The heat from the reactor water converts the external water into steam.

The reactor water then passes out of the generator and back into the reactor. The pressurised steam from the external water source travels from the exchanger to drive the turbines and generators that create the electricity. These are housed in a completely separate building to the nuclear reactor.

The reactor water and external water are segregated within the steam generator in two closed loops to prevent radioactive contamination.

On the night of 27th March 1979, one of the operatives in Reactor number 2 (TMI-2) at Three Mile Island noticed there was a blockage in the condensate polishers. These are sophisticated filters designed to eliminate any minerals or impurities being carried by the water into the steam generator and causing corrosion damage to that unit.

This common blockage problem with these resin filters was usually cleared with a blast of compressed air. On this occasion, it did not work. 'Plan B' was then put into action which was to blast the water with the compressed air using the hydraulic pressure created to shift the blockage materials.

Fortunately, this did the trick. Unfortunately, unknown to the workers, it had also forced a small amount of water through a check valve. This water then escaped into an instrument air line causing those instruments to malfunction.

At four the following morning the plant's computers detected the water causing the problem with the instruments. Within seconds, they had shut down the feed water pumps, condensate pumps and their boosters. This starved the reactor of its supply of coolant causing a rapid increase in heat and pressure. Sensing this, the reactor's computers performed an emergency shut down of the fission process within the reactor. The cadmium rods were then automatically inserted into the reactor to stop the nuclear chain reaction.

This triggered a number of alarms in the control room and control panel 'lit up like a Christmas tree' according to one witness. The three shift workers on duty obviously knew something was wrong but not *what* was wrong. This was a situation they had not been trained for and had never encountered before.

Although the chain reaction had now stopped, heat and pressure within the reactor continued to rise. At this stage, three auxiliary pumps automatically kicked in to provide coolant water to the reactor. They were designed to do this if the main pumps ceased to function as was the case in this incident. Had the auxiliary pumps performed as planned, that would have been the end of the matter.

At this point, a crucial failure to follow procedure escalated this minor industrial accident into a major disaster. The valves on the auxiliary pumps had been shut down for routine maintenance. To do this without shutting down the whole plant was strictly forbidden under the Nuclear Regulatory Commission's rules.

With the auxiliary pumps unable to pump any water into the reactor the dangerous rise in pressure and heat continued unabated. This rise in pressure within the reactor then triggered the relief valve situated at the top of its steel container causing coolant to pour out of the reactor and into an overflow tank. Once enough coolant had been released to stabilise the situation, the relief valve was designed to shut off. In the event, a mechanical fault caused it to jam open and an unrestricted flow of coolant flowed out of the reactor.

Unfortunately, the operators in the control room had no remote visibility of this valve such as closed circuit television. Had this been the case, they would have quickly seen that the valve was jammed open and taken appropriate action.

Instead they relied upon a warning light on the control panel to alert them to any problem with the pressure relief valve. When this switched off, the operators assumed the pressure relief valve had shut. In fact, when the warning light went dark it was simply indicating the message to shut the relief valve had been sent to the valve though not necessarily obeyed. It was, to put it mildly, a crucial design flaw.

Another problem with monitoring instruments was the fact that the level of coolant water within the reactor was not measured directly. Instead the instruments read the pressure inside the reactor interpreting this as the level of water coolant.

So, the uncontrolled rise of pressure in the reactor caused these instruments to deliver false readings to the control panel. Instead of indicating a dangerous loss of coolant, they showed the exact opposite, that the reactor housing was steadily filling up with coolant. In fact the instruments falsely showed the coolant water level reaching 400 inches. To allow the coolant to rise beyond this risked causing a catastrophic explosion within the reactor.

Fearing the emergency core cooling pumps that had started automatically, were forcing too much coolant into the reactor, the operators turned them off. They were not to know it, but this was exactly the wrong thing to do. With the reactor starved of coolant, what remained within its housing began to boil leading to the meltdown of the uranium fuel. The reactor was now effectively on fire and in danger of burning through the steel containment shell. If this happened, then molten radioactive fuel would continue to burn down into the ground below. This was known in the business as a China Syndrome.

This term was originally coined by Ralph E. Lapp, the nuclear physicist and author of '*The Voyage of The Lucky Dragon*'. Basically it was a metaphorical way of saying that should a reactor fire ever break out and was not stopped, it would burn down through the earth until it reached China. Whilst in reality, this was impossible the actual consequences of such a fire could be catastrophic.

In the case of Three Mile Island, if the melted fuel burned through the steel container it would carry on downwards until it reached the water table. On contact with this flow of molten uranium all groundwater in the immediate area of the plant would instantly turn to steam. There would then be a huge explosion followed by a series of many geysers of radioactive steam bursting out of the ground in an area up to twenty miles around the plant. One official estimate was that such an event would cost 40,000 lives.

Inside the reactor building, coolant water and steam continued to flow out of the faulty pressure valve. This filled the reactor building with a highly radioactive mixture of steam and water. At 4:11 a.m. the pressure relief tank that collected the water pouring out of the faulty valve then overflowed into the reactor chamber. This triggered an alarm. Inside the now crowded control room it was bedlam with alarms going off and the workers desperately trying to work out what was going wrong. This is probably why this particular alarm was ignored.

It took until 6 o'clock on the morning of 28th March 1979 for the full severity of the crisis to be realised by the new shift. By this time, 32,000 gallons of highly radioactive coolant water had leaked out seriously contaminating the whole reactor chamber.

At about 7:30 a.m. on 28th March, Gary Miller the Station manager declared a general emergency which had a 'potential for serious radiological consequences' to the general public. In other words there could be a serious leak of radiation contaminating the surrounding area. The owners of the plant Metropolitan Edison (Met Ed) immediately notified the Pennsylvania Metropolitan Emergency Agency (PEMA) who then contacted the State Governor's office. On receiving this alarming information, the State Governor Richard L. Thornborough tasked Deputy Governor William Scranton to gather as much information as he could about the accident.

The next few hours were characterised by a series of confusing and sometimes contradictory public statements about the ongoing accident. At an early press conference Scranton said there had been a small release of radiation from the plant with no overall increase in general radiation levels. Met Ed then contradicted this by saying there had been *no* release of radiation. In the event monitoring instruments at the plant showed that there had been a small release of radioactive particles.

Meanwhile, the Nuclear Regulatory Commission had sent two top officials from their HQ at Bethesda, Maryland to Three Mile Island to obtain a clear picture of the incident. They were the chairman of the NRC Joseph Hendrie and one of their commissioners Joseph Gilinsky. They were also hampered by a confused situation with conflicting sources of information.

In fact, by the time the NRC officials arrived at the plant, half the uranium within the reactor had already melted. Sixteen hours after the start of the emergency, the managers in the control room realised they had a loss of coolant accident in reactor 2. The primary loop pumps were activated and coolant was again pumped into the reactor. At last the pressure and heat within the stricken reactor began to drop and the dreaded China Syndrome was averted.

The emergency was far from over however. By the evening of 29th March, the reactor containment hall was awash with 100,000 gallons of radioactive water. This was creating a large amount of unstable gas which could have ignited releasing a large amount of radiation into the wider atmosphere.

To prevent this from happening, the plant's managers decided on a controlled release of part of this radioactive gas. On the following morning of Friday 30th 1979, The State Governor Dick Thornborough declared a state of emergency advising the evacuation of all children and pregnant women from a radius of five miles around the nuclear plant. This was then increased to 20 miles.

As loudspeaker trucks toured the area announcing the state of emergency, towns and villages such as Goldboro just across the river from Three Mile Island became ghost towns. Journalist and author of the book *Meltdown!* Wilborn Hampton recalled the surrealistic scenes of empty houses with their televisions still switched on and front doors left wide open. In fact, the total number of people who evacuated the area was 140,000.

Meanwhile, at the plant itself they were facing another potentially catastrophic hazard. A bubble of hydrogen created by the reactor fire had been detected within the reactor. It was feared that if this combined with oxygen, continued to expand, it could blow the reactor apart destroying the whole plant and covering the surrounding area in a deadly blanket of radioactivity. Immediate steps were taken to release the hydrogen gas from the reactor. By the next day, the bubble had shrunk significantly thus averting yet another domesday scenario, this time a hydrogen explosion.

Since the beginning of the incident U.S. President Jimmy Carter had been kept informed of events and had followed them closely. With a Batchelor of Science degree and working experience of nuclear energy from his time in the Navy, Carter was well aware of the potential danger of the situation if the accident at Three Mile Island got out of hand. Already concerned by the confused and contradictory messages coming out of the various press conferences, he decided that he and his wife Roselynn would visit the Plant as soon as possible.

This horrified his aides who felt it would place the Presidential couple in harms way unnecessarily. Radiation had already been detected in the control room outside the containment area. What if there was another more intense leak fatally injuring the President? Or what if he was trapped in the plant if and when the reactor actually exploded. To his credit, Carter stuck to his guns and on Sunday 1st April he and Roselynn took off from the White House Lawn in the Presidential Helicopter and headed towards Three Mile Island.

Later on that day, the President and his wife were filmed being shown round the plant by James Floyd, Director of Operations for the TMI - 2 reactor and in the company of Harold Denton, Head of the NRC and State Governor Dick Thornborough. This very public show of confidence from 'The Commander in Chief' and top officials went a long way to reduce public anxiety about the safety effects of the accident.

It was also a watershed moment marking the beginning of the end of America's worst nuclear accident. Over the following week, the damaged reactor was brought under control. As the radiation readings in the area surrounding the plant were revealed to be at very low and safe levels, residents began to return to their homes. By the end of April, 98% of the residents had returned. The authorities remained watchful and 250,000 bottles of potassium iodide, an anti-radiation drug to protect against thyroid cancer, was shipped in to nearby Harrisburg by The Food and Drug Administration in the event of a further radiation release.

Although The Three Mile Island accident resulted in no fatalities, there were many long term repercussions. It was marked up as a Level 5 Category Accident on the International Nuclear Event Scale making it a serious accident with wider consequences. In comparison, both the Fukushima and Chernobyl accidents were at Level 7, the highest rating on the INES scale.

The TMI-2 reactor was so severely damaged by the partial meltdown that it never operated again. It was decommissioned over a period of 13 years from 1980 to 1993. During this time all radioactive materials were removed including the fuel and 2.23 million gallons of contaminated water. The total cost of the decommissioning and clean up was $973 million dollars. This is far less than the cost of Chernobyl whose ongoing direct cost is estimated to be $235 billion dollars.

It should also be born in mind that, unlike Chernobyl, nobody was killed or injured by the Three Mile Island Accident and no land was lost to radiation. In contrast, the indirect costs of Chernobyl in terms of damage to the local agricultural industry, rehousing thousands of people displaced by the disaster and increased health care runs to many billions of dollars. This includes a thirty mile exclusion zone within which is the abandoned city of Pripyat. Eventual deaths from the accident are estimated to be between 4000 and 93,000 people.

In view of this, it is unfortunate that the political and economic repercussions of the Three Mile Island accident on the American nuclear industry have been so monumental. After the accident, the expansion of the U.S. nuclear power industry ground to a halt. This was because the accident gave great impetus to the anti-nuclear movement making the whole nuclear industry a pariah for the next thirty years. This was definitely helped by an eerie coincidence in which art imitated real life events.

Twelve days before the accident, the film *The China Syndrome* starring Michael Douglas Jane Fonda and Jack Lemmon was released. As its name suggests, this dark thriller dealt with an accident at a nuclear power plant that comes close to causing a reactor fire. It was strongly attacked as being a fictional hatchet job on the nuclear industry by its leaders at the time. However, much, though certainly not all, of the detail in the film matched what subsequently occurred in the Three Mile Island accident. The film won a Best Actor award on its release at the Cannes Film Festival for Jack Lemmon. It was also lauded by many critics and was a box office success. The way it shone a light on the nuclear industry and the fact that Fonda became a high profile anti-nuclear campaigner was clearly a P.R. disaster for the industry.

Following the Three Mile Island accident, of the 129 new nuclear plants approved for construction in the U.S., only fifty-three went ahead and were completed. Between 1980 and 1984, fifty-one nuclear power projects were cancelled.

The Chernobyl Disaster that occurred in 1986 delivered the final *coup de grace* to the expansion of nuclear power throughout the world. In September 2019, the Three Mile Island Nuclear Plant was finally closed. Reasons for the closure were high maintenance costs and cheaper energy sources such as natural gas and renewables. It had been argued by local politicians fighting to keep the plant open, that if nuclear energy received the same subsidies as its wind and solar counterparts it would be able to compete on a level playing field.

It is also worth remembering that Three Mile Island's other reactor had a truly exemplary safety record. Since it was commissioned in the mid 1970s TMI-1 ran its whole working life without incident.

A number of important lessons were learned from the Three Mile Island Accident. In March 1979, President Carter commissioned The Report of the President's Commission on the Accident at Three Mile Island (1979). This would highlight a number of areas where improvements to the safe operation of nuclear power plants could be made. In brief these are:

Improvement of Operator Training

The TMI accident exposed the lack of experience and knowledge of workers at Three Mile Island in initially dealing with the incident. This was compounded by their inability to actually see what was happening in the reactor hall. As a result, operatives are now trained on full scale simulators of nuclear plants. This training includes a wide range of accident scenarios.

Greater Interchange of Knowledge and Information.

As a direct result of the TMI accident, the Institute of Nuclear Power Operations and National Academy for Nuclear Training were established. These two linked bodies are dedicated to the pursuit of excellence and shared knowledge throughout the whole of the U.S.

Nuclear Industry. In the forty years since the accident this has led to a marked improvement in the safe, efficient and professional way U.S. Nuclear Power Plants are operated.

Faults in the Machine to Human Interface

One of the reasons for the severity of the TMI accident was the poor design of the control panel and its instruments. The operators' initial confusion and failure to identify that it was a loss of coolant accident was that the plant's control panel was not designed with humans in mind. Even with the benefit of hindsight this seems a particularly strange failing. It would certainly account for the confusing way the pressure valve warning light worked and the fact the operators could not actually see what was happening in the reactor room.

It was clearly a case of that very common failing that I call *The Curse of Presumed Prior Knowledge*. This occurs in a very wide variety of machines ranging from digital cameras to cars where the manufacturers automatically assume their new owners already know 25% of the way something works. In reality, you should always assume the operator of a new device knows nothing about it and must start from scratch (i.e. where is the on/off switch?).

Fortunately, in the case of nuclear power plants this lesson has been taken onboard. Nowadays, instrumentation in the control rooms is designed to convey information to the operators as quickly and clearly as possible.

Since Three Mile Island, there has not been a major incident involving a nuclear power plant in the United States. There have been no fatalities and no land has been irradiated.

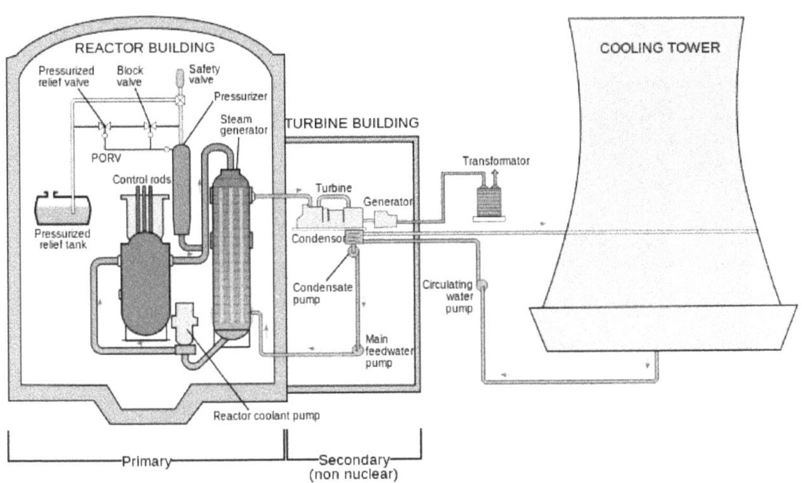

Diagram showing the layout of reactor TMI-2 at Three Mile Island nuclear power plant where the major accident occurred on 28th March 1979
Image courtesy Wikipedia

Three Mile Island Nuclear Power Plant after the accident showing Reactor 2 on the left hand side of the photograph.
Photograph by Z22/Wikipedia

President Jimmy Carter being shown round TMI -2 reactor on 1st April 1979. With him are left to right: Harold Denton, Governor Dick Thornburgh and James Floyd, supervisor of TMI-2 operations.
Photograph by John G Kemeny et al

Cleaning up radiation after the accident at Three Mile Island
Photograph by John G Kemeny et al

Chapter 13
Naval Nuclear Catastrophes

Since the early 1960s a number of nuclear powered submarines have come to grief. However, not all of these tragic accidents were due to either their nuclear power plants or weapons. Accordingly, this chapter will only deal with those accidents linked to a malfunction directly connected to the vessel's nuclear power plants or involving nuclear weapons on board these ships.

Submarine K19 'Hiroshima'
A Deadly Catalogue of Accidents
Northern Russia, Soviet Union
1958 - 2002

It seems that some ships are saddled with ill luck from their very inception. Submarine K-19, one the Soviet Union's two earliest nuclear submarines certainly seemed to fit this particular bill.

When the world's first nuclear submarine, *USS Nautilus* was launched on 21st January 1954, it became clear the Americans were way ahead of the Soviets in the naval arms race. Desperate to catch up, the Russians embarked on a hurried programme of developing their own nuclear submarines.

K-19, one of the first two Soviet nuclear submarines was constructed under this programme at Severodvinsk naval shipyard 22 miles outside the arctic city of Archangel. Between the initial laying down of her keel on 17th October 1958 and her completion in April 1959 no less than ten workers were killed in a number of accidents. However, these tragedies had nothing to do with bad luck and everything to do with the Soviet doctrine of adherence to the ideal of communist superiority overriding safety.

K-19's launch on 8th April 1959 was inauspicious to say the least. Breaking with seafaring tradition, a man rather than a woman was chosen to smash the celebratory bottle of champagne on the submarine. This honour fell to Captain 3rd Rank V. V. Panov. His champagne bottle struck the hull of the boat and failed to break. This was a very bad omen in seafaring terms.

From then on, the submarine was dogged by a number of problems relating either to human error or the vessel's hurried construction. These began in January 1960 when a reactor rod was bent due to improper operation. During her sea trials a number of incidents of varying severity also occurred.

Between July 1960 and 8th November 1960, K-19 travelled a total of 10,779 miles. All seemed well until the vessel surfaced. Then it was discovered that the rubber coating on the hull was faulty and had become detached.

After this was replaced, deep water trials to a depth of 300 metres (980 feet) commenced. During this trial dive severe flooding occurred in the reactor compartment. This forced K-19 to rapidly resurface. While doing this, the extra water from the flooding caused the vessel to nearly capsize. On this occasion, the cause of the flooding was traced to a faulty gasket left in place during construction.

In December 1960, a defective pump caused loss of coolant leading to a shutdown of one of the vessel's two nuclear power plants. Fortunately, the fault was rectified by seagoing repairs allowing K-19 to return safely to port.

In the summer of 1961 K-19 embarked on her maiden voyage with Captain Nikolai Vladimirovich Zateyev as her first commander. The total crew numbered 139 men including several officers sent along as observers.

On 4th July, K-19 was taking part in a major Soviet Naval exercise called *Operation Arctic Circle*. She was to play the role of a NATO submarine evading the Soviet forces. At 4:15 in the afternoon K-19 was off the south eastern coast of Greenland when pressure in the cooling system of the starboard reactor suddenly dropped to zero. This in turn knocked out the coolant pump. Deprived of the vital coolant, the reactor in the power plant began to heat up dangerously. The crew discovered this fault had been caused by a major leak in the coolant system.

Initially, Captain Zatayev tried contacting Moscow to request assistance. To his horror he discovered the long range radio system was not working. Apparently its aerials had been damaged by sea water ingress. From then on, he and his crew had to face this major emergency on their own. If they were unable to bring the situation under control, they faced the horrifying prospect of a nuclear blast destroying them and their submarine. The Captain also feared that such an explosion would damage a nearby NATO Base accidentally sparking a Third World War.

To prevent the reactor from overheating, the crew inserted control rods into the reactor to stop the chain reaction. This did not work and the temperature soared inexorably to 800 degrees centigrade.

It is fortunate that an individual as decisive and experienced as Zatayev was in charge since it was his and his crew's subsequent actions that prevented a much bigger disaster.

As soon as he realised the control rods were not working, Zatayev ordered the maintenance crew to construct a temporary cooling system. This meant the men had to work in an area of dangerously high radiation. Zatayev and his engineering crew knew this but to save their ship and the rest of the crew they did the job anyway. Apart from gas masks, raincoats and boots, they had no proper protective clothing. Mercifully the temporary cooling fix worked reducing the reactor temperature to safe levels. It would prove to be at a high human cost.

Indeed, all eight members of that engineering crew had died of radiation poisoning within a month of the accident.

Whilst the immediate threat of a catastrophic explosion had been averted, the rest of the crew were by no means out of the woods. The reason for this was the original reactor accident had caused radioactive steam to leak out into the vessel's ventilating system. This irradiated the rest of the submarine and her crew. Fifteen more crew members would die over the next two years from the effects of radiation poisoning.

Finally, K-19 rendezvoused with S-S70, a diesel powered Soviet submarine. She towed K-19 back to her home port in the White Sea. Before this happened, Zatayev was offered help by U.S. naval warships that had picked up distress signals. Fearing this might expose Soviet naval secrets to the Americans he declined their help.

Given K-19's dark history of accidents and fatalities, it is hardly surprising that she earned the nickname *Hiroshima* amongst submariners. What is surprising is that, following the accident off Greenland, she was not scrapped altogether.

In fact, the authorities saw fit to replace her two reactors sending her back into service once more. Like so much other Soviet military nuclear waste the scrapped reactors were dumped in the Kara Sea in Arctic Russia. There has subsequently been much international criticism of the haphazard way the Russians have disposed of this waste. Concern about the danger of wide scale radioactive contamination of neighbouring seas and oceans from this deadly submarine graveyard continues to this day.

If the Russian authorities thought that the recommissioning and upgrading of K-19 would turn a page on its tragic past, they were wrong. On 15th November 1969 K-19 collided with the American submarine *USS*

Gato that she was thought to be shadowing at a depth of 200 feet in the Barents Sea.

Whilst the American submarine continued on her way with little or no damage, K-19 sustained extensive nose damage. Her sonars were completely destroyed along with her forward torpedo tube covers. After resurfacing under emergency conditions the Russian submarine limped back to port.

Then in February 1972 when the K-19 was over three hundred feet below the North Atlantic a fire broke out when hydraulic fluid leaked onto a hot filter. The subsequent rescue operation by 30 Soviet Navy ships took forty days. The total death toll amongst the submarine's crew was thirty seamen.

Once again K-19 was patched up and put to sea where she suffered yet another fire in November 1972. Luckily this one was extinguished without injury or loss of life. The final incident in K-19's jinxed life occurred on 15th August 1982 when two sailors suffered severe burns from a short circuit. One survived whilst the other died after five days.

On 19th April 1990, this most unlucky of submarines was finally decommissioned. Four years later K-19 was transferred to the Soviet Navy repair yard of Polyarny on the Kola Bay in the Russian far north. In 2002 she was finally scrapped at the Nerpa Shipyard in Murmansk.

It took the Russian authorities many years to come completely clean about the full extent of the long running disaster that was K-19. What finally emerged in the era of *Glasnost* was a woeful tale of hurried and shoddy construction leading to a series of fatal and serious accidents.

As for Zatayev and his crew, they were sworn to secrecy for many years about the nuclear disaster off Greenland. However, on 6th August 1961, twenty six members of the crew were awarded medals for the courage and bravery during the accident.

It was not until after the fall of the Soviet Union that the tragic story of K-19 was finally told. In 1991 an article in *Pravda* related the story of the fated submarine from a Russian perspective.

Captain Zatayev also wrote the story of the nuclear accident in his memoirs which he published before his death in 1998. That was the first time he made his misgivings about the problems caused by the rushed nature of K-19's construction public.

His revelations were also used as one of the information sources for Katherine Bigelow's gripping film *K-19-The Widowmake*r. Although the film is largely an accurate account of the accident, it attracted criticism from some quarters for inaccuracies and fictionalisations of certain events. Apparently, the surviving submariners from K-19 were unhappy with the initial script they were shown. Accordingly, the moviemakers made some amendments.

It is fair to point out that Captain Peter Huchthausen (Retd) of the U.S. Navy on whose book the film was largely based, insisted that the finished production was a generally accurate recounting of the accident. In an interview on CNN's News in 2002 he insisted that the movie was a "pretty close" account of the Greenland incident. He also paid fulsome tribute to the Captain and crew of K-19 describing their actions when confronted by potential disaster as truly heroic.

The nickname *Widowmaker* was a fictional one thought up for the film since the real one - *Hiroshima* - could have caused offence to audiences for obvious historical reasons.

In 2006 Mikhail Gorbachev wrote a letter to the Norwegian Nobel Prize Committee recommending that the crew of K-19 be awarded the Nobel Peace Prize for their courageous actions in containing the accident.

The K-19 incident was by no means the only accident caused by a loss of coolant in a submarine's reactors. In October 1960 K-8, a November Class nuclear submarine belonging to the Soviet Northern Fleet was on exercises in the Barents Sea when she suffered a loss of coolant in her reactor.

The apparent cause was the rupturing of a steam generator tube. On this occasion a substantial amount of radioactive gas leaked out contaminating the whole vessel. Whilst there were no deaths, many of the crew were exposed to high levels of radiation with three suffering acute radiation sickness.

Ten years later K-8 was one of 80 other submarines taking part in one of history's biggest naval exercises. Lasting between April and May 1970, the Soviet Navy mounted Okean (Ocean) a naval exercise which also included 84 warships, 45 naval logistics and intelligence gathering vessels and several hundred aircraft. Spanning the North Atlantic, from the Russian Arctic down to the Bay of Biscay it was designed to demonstrate the strength of the Soviet Navy especially to the Americans.

Offensive attack exercises on naval vessels in the Atlantic were co-ordinated with similar 'attacks' in the North Pacific. It was truly a show of great strength telling the rest of the world that the Soviet Navy had arrived.

On April 8th K-8 was in the Bay of Biscay about 260 nautical miles off the coast of Spain when she suffered two serious simultaneous fires caused by the vessel's electrical system short circuiting. The fires spread rapidly through the submarine's air conditioning system. In an attempt to control the fires several compartments were sealed killing eight seamen inside them.

The fires had also forced the shut down of K-8's two nuclear reactors. Deprived of its main power, the Captain ordered the K-8 to surface and await the rescue vessels. In the meantime he ordered all the crew out of the submarine's interior.

When the salvage vessel arrived to take K-8 in tow, a senior officer ordered the crew back on board the submarine. Reluctantly, their commander Captain 2nd Rank Vsevolod Borisovich Bessonov took fifty-two of the crew back on board. As the submarine was being towed in rough seas back to her arctic base a further disaster overwhelmed her. Carbon monoxide poisoning killed all the crew who had been forced to re-board K-8. Seventy-three other crewmen who were not on board at the time survived.

In a final act of this maritime tragedy, K-8 was flooded by the stormy seas and sank to a depth of 15,350 feet (4,680 metres) in the Bay of Biscay. Those 52 submariners and four nuclear armed torpedoes are all encased within this watery tomb.

Sources

Soviet Navy Threatened U.S. in '70s With Boat Tech Advances (September 1972). Popular Mechanics October 2009.

OKEAN: A Massive Soviet Exercise, 50 Years Later By Norman Polmar April 2020 Proceedings U.S. Navy Institute.

Submarine K-11
Reactor Accident and Radiation Release
Severodvinsk, Archangel, Soviet Union
7th and 12th February 1965

Submarine K-11 was one of the Soviet Union's earliest nuclear submarines entering service in 1961. On 7th and 12th February 1965, this vessel suffered two separate reactor accidents in the arctic naval base of Severodvinsk near Archangel in Russia's far north.

Both incidents occurred during the removal of the reactor core and were caused by human error. On 7th February the lid on the reactor was removed without first securing the control rods. This led to an uncontrolled chain reaction causing an unplanned release of radioactive steam into the surrounding atmosphere.

With the threat of a major disaster occurring, all operations were suspended and personnel withdrawn from the affected area. An investigation was mounted over the next five days. No satisfactory conclusions were reached and the removal of the spent reactor was again attempted on 12th February. As in the earlier incident, the control rods were not secured. This led to a fire in the reactor and a further release of radiation. This forced a halt to the refuelling and the two damaged reactors were then removed and dumped in the neighbouring Kara Sea.

Seven men were subsequently treated for radiation sickness but no deaths relating to these accidents were recorded. After new reactors were installed K-11 went on to serve in the Soviet Northern Fleet for the next twenty-two years notching up over 220,000 miles. She was decommissioned in 1990 and has been laid up in Gremhika Bay in the Murmansk Oblast since 2000.

Sources

The Russian Northern Fleet Submarine Accidents Bellona Report number 2:96. Written by: Thomas Nilsen, Igor Kudrik and Alexandr Nikitin.

Project Azorian
North Pacific
8th March 1968 - 1974

The Kamchatka Peninsula is a long tongue of mineral rich land to the North of Vladivostok in Russia's Far East. Rybachly is a Russian Naval Base at Kamchatka's main city of Petrapavlovsk. In 1968, K-129, a Golf 2 Class diesel electric powered submarine was stationed there. Her sinking in the North Pacific in early spring 1968 led to one of the Cold War's most remarkable intelligence operations.

Although not a nuclear powered submarine K-129 was armed with three RN 21 nuclear missiles. These were the first Soviet weapons capable of being launched from a submarine with each warhead having the yield of 800 kilotons. The RN 21's operational range was 890 nautical miles (1,650 kms). As such, they were of considerable interest to the U.S. and the Western intelligence community.

K-129's last mission out of Petropavlovsk was to patrol an area of the Pacific to the Northwest of the Hawaiian Islands. In the event of war breaking out between Russia and America, she would launch her nuclear missiles at U.S. targets from this location. She never completed this last mission.

On 8th March 1968, K-129 disappeared with all 98 crew in the Northern Pacific somewhere north west of the Hawaiian Island chain. After a number of failed attempts to contact the submarine, the Soviet High Command announced that K-129 had been lost presumed sunk. The Russians launched a major air/sea search for the missing vessel without success. After two months of fruitlessly scouring the vastness of the Northern Pacific, they called off the search.

Meanwhile, alerted by the Soviet announcement of the lost submarine and their subsequent search, the U.S. Navy began to investigate further. To do this they enrolled the audio specialists of the U.S. network of hydrophones in the Northern Pacific called SOSUS (Sound Surveillance System). This undersea monitoring system was primarily used to keep track of Soviet and Chinese submarines. In this case they were searching for an auditory clue as to the fate of K-129. Sure enough on the recording for 8th March 1968, SOSUS hydrophones had recorded a large explosion in the vicinity of where K-129 went missing. This marked the beginning of one of the most extraordinary episodes of the submarine Cold War.

Aware that K-129 had advanced RD 21 nuclear missiles on board, the CIA hatched a daring plan to lay hands on them. In July of that year, the Agency initiated a project to locate the sunken Soviet submarine. Called *Operation Sand Dollar* it involved sending *USS Halibut*, the U.S. Navy's only specialist deep search submarine to hunt for the wreck in the Northern Pacific. To accomplish this task, *Halibut* carried an array of remote controlled cameras.

On 20th August 1968 *USS Halibut* managed to locate the wreck of K-129. at a depth of 16,500 feet (4,900 metres) 1560 miles to the North West of Hawaii. She then spent the next few weeks taking no less than 20,000 close-up photographs of the wrecked Soviet submarine. The news of this discovery lit up the American intelligence community. The CIA began planning the second part of their project to obtain the Soviet missiles. This would involve retrieving the whole submarine from the sea bed and would become known as Project Azorian.

Despite the difficulty of recovering a sunken vessel from a depth of over three miles, the CIA were determined to try. With the authorisation of both President Nixon and the Secretary of Defense, Project Azorian was born. Its sole purpose would be to salvage the wreckage of submarine K-129 or, more importantly, the three nuclear missiles from the wreck. Due to its great secrecy, this salvage operation would be a CIA 'Black Operation' without the involvement of the U.S. Navy.

An indication of this operation's importance to the U.S. Government, was the fact it had a salvage vessel specially built for the project. It was called the *Hughes Glomar Explorer* (HGE) and was constructed with the involvement of reclusive billionaire Howard Hughes at a cost of $350 million ($1.4 Billion in 2020 values).

With such a price tag, the *Glomar Explorer* was a remarkable ship indeed. The cover story put out to the press by Howard Hughes was that this vessel had been developed to mine manganese nodules from deep seabeds. Since large deposits of these minerals were known to exist in The Northern Pacific, this was a perfectly feasible idea. Hughes' company already had a good working relationship with the intelligence community and he was only too happy to indulge in this subterfuge.

Glomar was built at the Sun Shipbuilding and Dry Dock company's yard in Chester, Pennsylvania over four years in conditions of great secrecy. Her keel was laid in the yard on 16th November 1971 and she was launched on 4th November 1972. This ship was constructed with a special grabbing mechanism to retrieve K-129 from the depths of the Pacific. To accomplish this, a large grappler affectionately nicknamed *Clementine* would be lowered to the ocean floor and literally grasp the submarine. To lower the grappler three miles down, 590 x 30 foot steel pipes would be gradually added in what was known in the drilling business as a 'string'.

The grabber claw and its driving mechanism was installed completely undercover. Then, to further defeat any prying eyes, it was installed in the *Glomar Explorer* from beneath her hull using a sunken barge.

This was accomplished by raising it through the ship's "moon pool". This is a large opening in the base of a ship's hull. Also known as a "wet porch" it allows salvaged objects to be safely brought on board a vessel without having to haul them over the ship's side. This avoids the risk of destabilising or even capsizing a ship in rough weather. In the case of *Glomar Explorer*, it was the only way to bring a wreck the size of K-129 on board. Whilst moon pools are usually open to the ocean, Glomar Explorer's had large doors that could be closed.

The building of *HGE* was a long saga of constant modifications, sharply rising costs followed by near cancellations by various secret committees. Added to this was the rapidly changing political landscape of The Watergate Scandal and President Nixon's ultimate resignation. The fear of some form of drastic, possibly military action by the Soviets if they discovered the project also weighed on some military minds.

In spite of this, Project Azorian did survive and on 4th November 1972 the *Glomar Explorer* was launched with a bottle of champagne smashed against her bow. To the outside world, she was the latest wonder in cutting edge deep sea mining technology.

At four thirty on the afternoon of 11th August 1973 the *Hughes Glomar Explorer* set sail from Hamilton, Bermuda where she had been completing months of exhaustive trials. She was finally on her way to do the job she had been built for. However, due to the fact she was too large to pass through the Panama Canal this involved an initial marathon voyage of over 15,000 miles.

The first 12,700 miles from Pennsylvania round South America through the Straits of Magellan to Long Beach California took 50 days. During that time she docked at Valparaiso in Chile to take on some crew whilst Allende's Government was toppled in a coup. Ironically, this was one CIA operation that had no involvement in that event.

On 20th June 1974, after further trials, the *Hughes Glomar Explorer* set out from Long Beach, California on the 3008 mile journey to the K-129 wreck site in the Northern Pacific. Appropriately, she arrived there on 4th July 1968, Independence Day, and was put to work under the direction of her CIA masters.

Salvaging an object, particularly one as large as a submarine weighing 1,750 tons, from the seabed at a depth of over three miles had never been attempted before. Retrieving K-129 involved gradually lowering *Clementine* to the sea bed by adding one 30 foot length of steel pipe after another through *Glomar Explorer's* moon pool. Once the submarine had been captured by the grabber claw, the whole process would be reversed drawing K-129 back to the surface.

Nothing is totally secret in our interconnected world and that included Operation Azorian. In the case of the Soviets, they had actually got wind of this salvage attempt by their American rivals **(2)**. As luck would have it, the Soviet Military top brass dismissed the idea as impossible.

This was greatly to the frustration of veteran Russian diplomat Anatoly Dobrynin, their ambassador to the UN. He made repeated frantic efforts to alert the Soviet military that a clandestine American salvage effort was afoot. Whilst not dismissing Dobrynin's warnings entirely, the military were at best sceptical about such an attempt. This scepticism must partly have been down to the fact that the Russian Navy's attempts to find K-129 had ended in failure. Later it would emerge this was because they had been searching in the wrong area of the Pacific.

A general order was put out to any Soviet ships to keep an eye out for unusual activity by the Americans. This may well have been why two Soviet Naval ships actually visited the *Glomar Explorer's* site during salvage operations. One of these ships was *Chazma* a missile range instrumentation vessel and the other was an oceanographic tug called *SB10*.

Arriving in the afternoon of 18th July, *Chazma* spent the next few hours closely observing and photographing the *Glomar*. She also launched her ship's helicopter to fly around the salvage vessel taking yet more photographs. Then, after interrogating the *Glomar's* captain as to what they were doing there ('deep sea mining' was the reply) she left for her home base at Petropavlovsk.

The *SB10* tug arrived on the morning of 22nd July and stayed considerably longer. Until she finally departed in the evening of 6th August, the tug kept a constant watch on the *HGE* sometimes coming as close as 75 yards from the vessel. In total the surveillance by the two Soviet vessels lasted 13 days and 16 hours. However, it seems they were unable to detect the true nature of the operation. During this time, in the evening of 1st August, the remains of the submarine were finally lifted from the ocean floor.

At this stage it seemed that the mission would be a complete success. Then, half way to the surface disaster struck when the submarine broke in two. The salvage crew could only look on in frustration as the lost section fell back to the ocean floor. It was especially disappointing to know that it contained those crucial RB 21 nuclear missiles.

In the murky world of espionage nobody can be quite sure if this is actually the case or yet another CIA cover story. After all, if they had managed retrieve the top secret Soviet missiles, the CIA would hardly announce it to the world. Interestingly, the official account of Project Azorian on the CIA website makes no mention of any attempted recovery of Soviet nuclear weapons (1). Another semi-official account of Project Azorian written by an anonymous member of its team and published in the journal *'Studies In Intelligence'* (1985) not only omits mention of recovering any Soviet nuclear weapons but also of the alleged loss of half the submarine. According to most accounts, the salvaged section contained only two nuclear armed torpedoes and the remains of six Russian seamen. Frustratingly, the real prize, the RB 21 missiles were in the lost section of the submarine.

In a poignant ceremony aboard the *Glomar Explorer*, these crew men were given a respectful burial at sea which included the Soviet anthem and their coffins draped in their country's flag. In 1992, a video shot of this ceremony was presented to Boris Yeltsin as a goodwill gesture by Robert Gates the Head of the CIA who was visiting Russia at the time.

A second salvage mission was planned by the CIA to recover the second section of K-129 that had slipped their grasp. Once again, that fickle Lady Fate would thwart their efforts. In July 1974, a batch of confidential documents were stolen during a break in at one of the Hughes Company's offices. Since some of these papers contained sensitive information linking Howard Hughes to Project Azorian, the CIA requested the help of the FBI in recovering them. Possibly not fully appreciating the highly delicate nature of these documents, the FBI enlisted the services of the Los Angeles Police Department.

Inevitably, information about Project Azorian then leaked into the public domain. Initially William Colby was successful in preventing any news of Project Azorian being published. In February 1975 journalist Seymour Hersh planned to publish an article about the project in *The New York Times*. Bill Kovach, the Washington chief of the newspaper heeded Colby's request to delay publishing the article until after Azorian was complete.

However all this was in vain when *The Los Angeles Times* made the story public. This was followed up by a television report on the Project by investigative reporter Jack Anderson. Although the media gave the project the incorrect name of *'Jennifer'*, the damage was done and the *Hughes Glomar Explorer's* cover was well and truly blown.

To thwart any further attempts by the CIA to recover the rest of K-129, the Soviet Navy stationed a vessel permanently at the wreck site. Sadly, that remarkable salvage ship *The Hughes Glomar Explorer, was* now robbed of her *raison d'etre*, making her effectively redundant.

After some unsuccessful attempts to sell her, the *Glomar Explorer* was mothballed at Suisan Bay in California. In spite of her unique ability to recover huge weights from extreme depths she proved too expensive for even the largest company to purchase and maintain. It seemed this remarkable ship who had served her nation so well was destined to fade into obscurity eventually to be scrapped.

However, after 25 years in mothballs, *Glomar Explorer* was refurbished and converted into a deep sea drilling rig at a cost of $180 million. Reflagged as *GSF Explorer*, she performed this role for Transocean, her new owners until 2015 when she was finally scrapped. Ironically, her last destination was a breakers yard in Zhoushan, The People's Republic of China - the only other country known to have secretly recovered a sunken submarine.

Footnote
The Raising of HMS Poseidon

On a bright clear day in June 1931, Royal Navy submarine *HMS Poseidon* was conducting exercises in the Yellow Sea off Weihai, China. In spite of excellent visibility, she managed to collide with a Chinese merchant ship, the *SS Yuta*. Thirty one of her crewmen managed to escape by diving into the sea before the submarine sank in 130 feet (40 metres) of water. This tragic incident only took minutes to act out but in that time it claimed the lives of twenty-one of the submarine's crew.

In 1972, the Communist Chinese navy managed to retrieve the Poseidon using their newly formed undersea recovery unit in a secret operation. Why they would want to salvage a forty-three year old British submarine remains a mystery. Perhaps it was just practice for their fledgling undersea recovery unit. On the other hand, in the early seventies, Mao's China was technologically quite backward, so even pre-war British marine engineering might have been useful to them. Whatever the reason, the clandestine raising of the Poseidon is the only case of its kind besides Project Azorian.

Sources

https://www.cia.gov/about-cia/cia-museum/experience-the-collection/index.html#!/story/14
1) Studies in Intelligence, Centre for The Study of Intelligence 1985

Footnote
Crazy Ivan

Throughout the Cold War, the opposing navies of NATO and the Warsaw Pact played risky games of cat and mouse beneath the world's oceans. This often involved the submarines of each side tailing one another at distances as close as a hundred feet. A common practice would be to follow the target submarine in what is known as its baffles. This is the area directly behind the stern of a submarine or ship which is an auditory dead zone where the vessel's sonar is unable to 'hear' the pursuing submarine's engines.

Both NATO and Soviet submarines employed tactics to throw off the pursuing submarines. One of the most common baffle clearing manoeuvres is for a submarine to turn sharp right or left and then sit and listen for the engine noise of a pursuing submarine. Another is known as '*Angles and Dangles*' in which the quarry submarine would go through a series of sudden turns and figures of eight. These manoeuvres would often be performed over an extended period making the submarine hard to follow.

All of these evasive tactics increased the risk of collision with the pursuing submarine, none more so than the one adopted by Russian submarines. This involved the submarine suddenly turning 180 degrees and then travelling directly towards the following submarine. Because it often involved head-on collisions with Soviet and NATO submarines it soon became known as *The Crazy Ivan* manoeuvre. On at least one occasion it was accompanied by the release of a torpedo which seriously damaged a nuclear submarine of a leading NATO navy.

With the introduction of sonar towed behind a vessel in what is known as a towed array, following submarines in their baffles is no longer an effective manoeuvre.

USNS Hughes Glomar Explorer.
US Navy Photograph

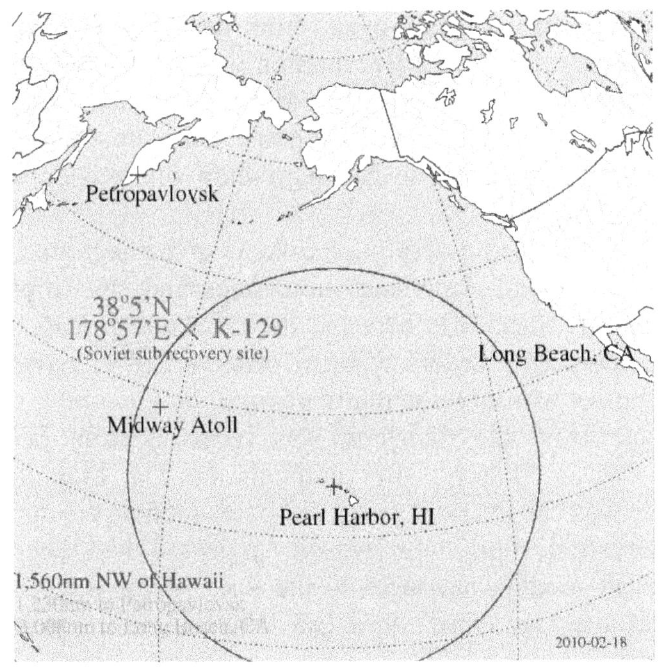

Map showing location of the wreck of Soviet submarine K-129 in the Northern Pacific.
Map by Enemenemu/Wikipedia

The Scorpion Mystery
The Sinking of the USS Scorpion
Atlantic Ocean off the Azores
22nd May 1968

1968 was a bad year for the world's navies with the loss of four submarines in unknown circumstances. On 25th January, the Israeli diesel electric sub *INS Dakar* sank in the Mediterranean with the loss of all sixty-nine crew. It's wreck was only located thirty-one years later lying between the islands of Cyprus and Crete. Why she sank remains a mystery.

Two days later on 27th January the French submarine *Minerve* disappeared just 28 miles from her home base in Toulon. All fifty-two crew were lost and the wreck was eventually found in deep waters in 2019. As with the *Dakar*, the cause of the sinking was unknown. On 8th March the Russian diesel electric submarine K-129 sank in the deep waters of the Northern Pacific off the Hawaiian island of Oahu. All ninety-eight members of her crew were lost.

Then on 22nd May 1968, USS Scorpion went down in the Atlantic off the Azores with the loss of all ninety-nine crew. One of two nuclear submarines lost by the U.S. Navy (The other was the *Thresher*), the cause of her sinking is unknown and a matter of much speculation.

The Scorpion set out on her final voyage from her home base of Norfolk Virginia on 15th February 1968. Her mission was to deploy with the U.S. Sixth Fleet in the Mediterranean. On 16th May, she headed out of the Mediterranean into the Atlantic for the voyage home. En route, the sub put into the U.S. Naval Base of Rota in Spain to drop off two crew members.

This part of the Atlantic was a very busy Cold War 'battleground' at this time with both Soviet and American submarines and spy ships watching each other closely. Stand-offs between the rival naval vessels were not uncommon. *Scorpion's* orders were to observe Soviet naval activity off the nearby Azores whilst on the return voyage.

The last message from the *Scorpion* was received from her Commanding Officer, Francis Slattery, after midnight on 21st May. It stated that the submarine was closing on a group of Soviet submarines and vessels for close observation. For some reason, *Scorpion* had been experiencing difficulties in sending messages to the Rota Naval Base in Spain. Instead, that final message came via a U.S. Naval listening post near Nea Makri in Greece.

After days of silence, the U.S. Navy launched a search for the *Scorpion* on the assumption she was missing. On 5th June 1968, the U.S. Navy made the terrible announcement that *USS Scorpion* and her ninety-nine crew were 'presumed lost'. As well as a great tragedy, this was also a 'Broken Arrow' incident. On board the submarine were two Mark 45 torpedoes armed with W34 nuclear warheads.

Brought into service in 1959, the twenty foot long Mark 45 was a wire guided torpedo designed to attack fast enemy submarines at great depths. The W34 was an eleven kiloton nuclear bomb primarily designed for use in such deep sea weapons.

An intensive search for the submarine continued throughout the summer and autumn. Concentrating on the Atlantic area near the Azores, it had two prongs. On the one hand there was a team led by Dr John P. Craven based at the undersea listening post he had established on the Canary Islands. Craven was the Chief Scientist of the Navy's Special Projects Division. That unit's speciality was finding lost objects at sea using The Bayesian search method (*See Palomares B-52 Nuclear Incident*).

Then there was the *USS Mizar* an oceanographic research vessel that had been used in two previous undersea naval searches. These were successful in locating the submarine *USS Thresher* in 1964 and the search for the nuclear bomb dropped off Palomares, Spain in 1966.

In late October 1968, with the aid of an underwater camera towed on a sled, she also found sections of the *Scorpion* at a depth of 9,800 feet (3000 metres) on the sea bed. The location was 400 nautical miles south west of the Azores. In addition to this, the U.S. Navy released some chilling audio tapes containing the actual sound of the *Scorpion* imploding under extreme water pressure. These were obtained by the system of static undersea listening devices established by the U.S. Navy to keep tabs on Soviet submarine activity known as Sound Surveillance System or SOSUS (*See also K-129 and Project Azorian*).

Dr Craven's team had also obtained very similar recordings from their listening post on the Canaries.

The subsequent Naval Court of Enquiry into the *Scorpion* tragedy was convened shortly after her loss. It's President was Vice Admiral Bernard L. Austin who had also presided over the *Thresher* enquiry. The Court's findings made public on 31st January 1969, ruled out sabotage but was unable to provide any one conclusive reason for the sinking of the *Scorpion*.

Since then, numerous theories about the cause of the submarine's tragic loss have been aired. These range from an explosion caused by a build up of hydrogen (1) to a catastrophic accident involving a torpedo.

The Court of Inquiry actually floated the theory that one of the submarine's non nuclear Mark 37 torpedoes was accidentally fired. It then homed in on its nearest target being the *Scorpion* with disastrous results. Another theory was that the silver-zinc batteries in one of the torpedoes overheated causing the weapon to explode (2).

At least two investigative books have come up with the most controversial theory that *USS Scorpion* was actually sunk by a Soviet submarine. Both *All Hands Down* by Kenneth Sewell and Jerome Preisler and *Scorpion Down* by Edward Offley (3) put forward this theory in ways that often read more like Cold War thrillers. Anyone who is tempted to think the idea of such an attack is too far fetched should look at recent history.

In 1978, Soviet air defences shot down a Korean passenger airliner and then another in 1983. On both occasions, the Korean planes had accidentally veered into Russian air space.

On 11th February 1992, U.S. nuclear submarine *Baton Rouge* was severely damaged when it collided with Russian nuclear submarine *Kostroma*. The incident occurred 12 miles off the Russian coast near Kildin Island north of Murmansk. Whilst the Russians claimed *Baton Rouge* was within their territorial waters the Americans have always asserted their vessel was in international waters. The jury is out over whether the collision was accidental or a deliberate ramming. *The Baton Rouge* was sufficiently badly damaged to be taken out of service in September 1993.

The second collision between an American and Russian submarine occurred just a year later on March 20th 1993. Once again it happened in the Russian Arctic just off the Kola Peninsula. This time the *USS Grayling* and the Russian nuclear submarine *Novomoskovsk* collided almost head on although the damage was much less than in the previous incident.

It should be pointed out that on both occasions, the U.S. submarines were conducting surveillance of the Russian submarine fleet very close to their territory. Furthermore, the Russians claimed the American subs were within their territorial limit of twelve miles. The U.S. has always denied this. Like the Russians the Americans observe a twelve mile territorial limit around their coasts.

While both collisions took place after the fall of the Soviet Union when Boris Yeltsin had come to power, Cold War paranoia and deep suspicion of the West persisted within the Russian military. This has certainly not lessened during the long rule of Vladimir Putin.

At the end of the day these many theories are just that - theories not facts. The truth lies hidden with *USS Scorpion* and her crew nearly two miles beneath the Atlantic waves.

USS Scorpion being launched at Groton, Connecticut, on 19th December 1959.
Photograph by US Navy

Sources

1) *Against The Tide* by Rear Admiral Dave Oliver.
(2) *Blind Man's Bluff: The Untold Story of American Submarine Espionage* (ISBN 0-06-103004-X) by Sherry Sontag, Christopher Drew, and Annette Lawrence Drew, published in 1998 by Public Affairs Press.
(3) *Scorpion Down* by Edward Offley. Basic Books ISBN 13: 9780641944642).

Footnote
The Mysterious sinking of the Dakar and Minerve January 1968

The loss of a submarine at sea with all hands is a particularly poignant tragedy. It contains all the elements of great disaster; the death of fifty to one hundred people in frightening circumstances, the mystery of the actual accident and the devastating impact on the bereaved families. This certainly applies to the loss of all those submarines in 1968.

INS Dakar (Hebrew for Swordfish) began life as Royal Navy submarine *HMS Totem* when she was launched in 1943. After the Second World War she was modified to travel faster and quieter. In 1965, *Totem* was sold along with her two sister submarines *Truncheon* and *Turpin* to the Israeli Navy .

At a ceremony at Portsmouth Naval Base on 10th November 1967 *HMS Totem* became *INS Dakar* of the Israeli Navy. After sea trials off the Scottish coast, *INS Dakar* left Portsmouth on 9th January 1968 for Haifa, Israel via Gibraltar. The plan was for her to travel at snorkel depth across the Mediterranean to her home port of Haifa. During the voyage her commander Major Ya'acov Ra'anan reported the vessel was making excellent progress and requested to dock at Haifa on 28th January 1968. This request was denied since the welcoming ceremony was already set up.

At 06:10 a.m. on 24th January 1968 *Dakar* broadcast her position as close to the eastern coast of Crete. She made a further two routine transmissions, the last of which was at 00:02 on 25th January 1968 . After that there was silence. Crucially, the last two transmissions did not give her position; *Dakar* had vanished.

Following a British Admiralty announcement on 26th January that *Dakar* was missing 100 miles west of Cyprus, a massive search was launched. Ships from the navies of Israel, the United States, Greece, Turkey, Great Britain and Lebanon scoured the Mediterranean for the next five days without success. The Israeli Navy continued the search alone from 31st January until 4th February 1968. During the search, there was just one glimmer of hope when a distress signal was picked up in Cyprus on 27th January from *INS Dakar*'s emergency buoy to the South East of the island. However, this was a single 'cry in the dark'.

The disappearance of the submarine occurred at a time of heightened tension in the Middle East. Following the Six Day War between Israel and her Arab neighbours in June 1967, the two sides remained at daggers drawn. This was known as The War of Attrition in which mainly the Egyptian Army fought a series of limited engagements with Israeli Forces. Speculation was rife that the Israeli submarine had been sunk by hostile action.

One story about the *Dakar*'s fate emanated from a member of the Egyptian military called Major Mohammed Azab who claimed the submarine had sunk following an engagement with an Egyptian Navy frigate, However, this story was treated with scepticism even in the higher echelons of the Egyptian Navy. It was also disproved by subsequent events.

The Israeli military denied the submarine had been sunk as a result of hostile action. A spokesman claimed that the submarine had been performing crash diving exercises when a mechanical malfunction caused it to sink to the seabed far beyond the *Dakar's* safe depth. In truth, nobody knew precisely why or how the submarine had come to grief. This was reflected in the generalised nature of the official Israeli government statement that the submarine sank due to 'technical or human malfunctioning and not foul play'.

Over a year after her disappearance, a fisherman found the emergency buoy marker from the stern of the submarine on a beach at Khan Younis in the Gaza Strip. A section of the cable that attached the buoy to the submarine was still fixed to the marker. The experts who examined these items wrongly concluded that the *Dakar* had sunk 50 - 70 miles (93-139 kilometres from her actual route. As a result many search expeditions over the next three decades failed to find the submarine because they were looking in entirely the wrong place.

Meanwhile, the rabbinical authorities had the complicated problem that, because the submarine had vanished at sea, all or some of the crew members could not be considered officially dead. This could only be accepted if all the men who had perished were buried in Israel. Because there was the extremely remote possibility the submarine had been captured, some or all the crew could be still alive and in captivity. This prevented some of the widows of the crew being able to remarry under Jewish/Israeli Law. The conundrum was finally resolved in 1981 when the

Chief Rabbi Shlomo Goren, who was chief military chaplain at the time, accepted a naval board of enquiry conclusion that all the crew had perished when the submarine sank (1). After thirteen years, this opened the way for the widows of crew members to remarry.

The wreck of *INS Dakar* was eventually located on 24th May 1999, thirty-one years after she sank. She was found by a U.S.-Israeli search mission using underwater search equipment such as the remotely operated submersible *Remora II.* The operation was led by Thomas Kent Detweiller an experienced specialist in nautical search and recovery. The submarine lies at a depth of 3,000 metres (9,800 feet) on the seabed between the islands of Crete and Cyprus.

Whilst the discovery brought some form of closure to the bereaved families of the crew, issues unique to Israel remain to be resolved. A burial ceremony over the wreck site has been performed; however since Judaic Law in Israel only recognises burial on land and not at sea this is not officially recognised. One solution has been considered though not enacted on to date. This is the recovery of the crew's remains so they can be buried on land. Even with the discovery of *INS Dakar*, the precise cause of her sinking remains a mystery.

Just two days after the loss of *INS Dakar,* the French submarine *Minerve* disappeared with all fifty-two hands only 46 kilometres (28 miles) from her home base of Toulon on the Southern French coast. She was travelling at snorkel depth in very heavy seas at the time. Her last message was to a Breguet *Atlantic* maritime patrol aircraft at 7:55 in the morning of 27th January 1968. It was a routine message by the Captain of the submarine André Fauve that *Minerve* would be at her home base within an hour. That was the last anyone heard from the submarine.

Shortly after her disappearance, a large scale air/sea search was mounted in the northern Mediterranean. Search vessels included the aircraft carrier *Clemenceau* and the remarkable deep sea submersible vehicle, *SP350 Denise.* This was operated by its inventor, the world renowned deep sea explorer Jaques Cousteau. In spite of this, the search yielded nothing and was called off on 2nd February 1968. Another search mission under the name *Operation Reminer* involving US Naval Survey Ship *Mizar* and another deep sea submersible *Archimède* continued the search until its conclusion in 1969 with no results.

Launched in 1961 *Minerve* was by no means an old submarine and her skipper André Fauve was an experienced submariner; at the time of the sinking, he had 7,000 hours experience underwater in submarines with no problems. The possible cause of the accident remained a mystery with the bad weather cited as a possible factor. At the time, *Minerve* was the only wrecked submarine of a Western navy that had not been located since the Second World War.

After pressure from the crew's bereaved families led by Hervé Fauve, the son of the Minerve's commander , the French Government began a new search on 4th July 2018. This mission used the oceanic search ship *Seabed Constructor* as its main vessel and Texas based company *Ocean Infinity.* Wall Street financier and investor Victor Vescovo loaned his deep sea submersible *Limiting Factor* to the operation.

Minerve was finally located on the seabed in the Gulf of Lion on 22nd July 2019 fifty-one years after she sank. The wreck is at a depth of 2,350 m (7,710 ft) and is broken into three sections. On 2nd February 2000 Hervé Fauve, the son of the submarine's commander accompanied by Victor Vescovo visited the wreck of Minerve to place a granite memorial next to the submarine whilst a recording of *'La Marseillaise'* was played. The site is now a marine sanctuary.

The probable cause of the tragedy has yet to be ascertained.

Map showing approximate location of the wreck of *USS Scorpion* lying at a depth of 9,800 feet (3,000 metres) 400 nautical miles (740 kilometres) south west of the Azores.
Map courtesy of Google

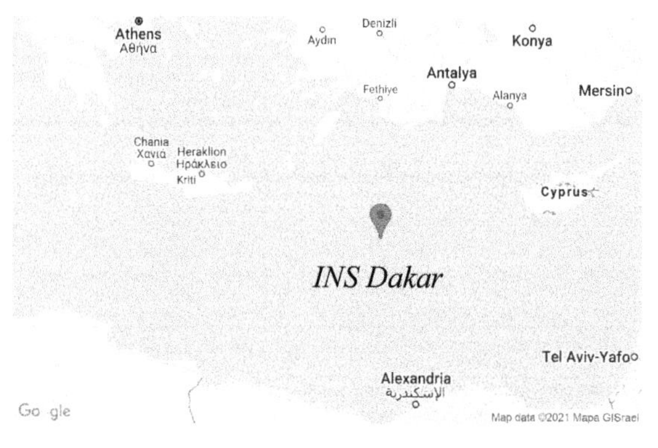

Map showing location of the wreck of the Israeli submarine *INS Dakar* mid way between Crete and Cyprus.

Map showing location of the wreck of the French Navy submarine *Minerve* in the Mediterranean 45 kilometres from her base at Toulon.
Maps created by Nick Brazil using Google

Submarine K-27
The Tragedy of 'The Little Golden Fish'
Reactor Failure and Severe on board Radiation Leak
24th May 1968

There is an old Russian fairytale about a wondrous little fish made completely of gold. In addition to this, the fish has the magical ability to grant you anything you wish for. The name of the fish is *'Zolotaya Rybka'* which in english means *Little Golden Fish*.

After five years in construction, Soviet nuclear submarine K-27 was launched at the Severodvinsk shipyard in the far north of Russia on 1st April 1962. Unlike the many other nuclear submarines that were constructed at that vast yard, K-27 had a crucial difference. Her two reactors were cooled not by water but by a liquid metal coolant made up of lead and bismuth. The main advantage of this type of coolant is that it has a very high boiling point allowing it to operate in a reactor at extremely high temperatures without the risk of a meltdown. In theory this meant the submarine's power plant was much more efficient.

The downside to this was it made the submarine very costly and slow to build. No wonder this experimental vessel which seemed to swallow up endless quantities of cash earned the nickname *'Little Golden Fish'*.

After eventually being launched in October 1963, K-27 was taken into the 17th Submarine Division of The Soviet Northern Fleet on 7th September 1965. Her home base was at Gremikha on the Kara Sea in the far north of The Soviet Union.

During her first five years, K-27's reactors proved to be temperamental and prone to faults. In spite of this she remained in active service. On 24th May 1968, K-27 was on a five day trip in the Arctic to test all the submarine's systems for a much longer seventy day underwater mission. It was then that her 'number came up' and disaster struck.

Twenty-two year old Vyacheslav Mazurenko, Chief Warrant Officer on the submarine remembered how the disaster unfolded. He was in the compartment that was next to the one that housed K-27's two reactors when he heard sounds of commotion and people running. The radiation supervisor who was also in the cabin, switched on the room's radiation sensor. To his horror, it immediately started beeping frenetically with readings going off the scale. As they had not been given adequate training, the other crew members did not fully understand what was happening.

In fact, one of the reactors had suffered a sudden and severe malfunction. For some unknown reason, power in this reactor dropped sharply and a deadly cocktail of radioactive gases were released into the engine room and the rest of the submarine. But Mazurenko and the rest of the crew were unaware of this since the gases were colourless and odourless.

After two hours some crew members were carried out of the reactor compartment suffering extreme fatigue. Even when this happened, Mazurenko thought it was probably down to exhaustion. Hell! Weren't they all tired all the time on these long voyages? The men weren't simply exhausted, they had acute radiation sickness from which they would not recover.

For several hours nine crew members battled unsuccessfully to rectify the failure. The reactor had been ruptured beyond repair by a partial coolant failure. By the time those men ceased their attempts to repair the reactor they had received fatal doses of radiation from a deadly mixture of gamma rays, thermal neutrons as well as alpha and beta radioactivity.

Forced to surface, K-27's Captain, Pavel Leonov received orders from base to hold his position and await further orders. Knowing this could take many hours during which time the crew would have died of radiation poisoning, he decided to ignore the order. He instructed his crew to return to base and for the next five hours the severely damaged sub limped back to Gremikha.

It was a homecoming that Vyacheslav Mazurenko vividly remembered with no fondness. As K-27 approached the dock at the base, emergency radiation alarms were sounding off causing the workers and their officers to flee in panic. It was as if the crew of the K-27 were manning a death ship, which indeed they were. When Mazurenko related his experiences of the disaster to the BBC in 2013 only 56 of the original crew of 144 were still alive.

After that fateful return to base, K-27 was moored up at Gremikha whilst the powers that be decided what to do with her. One plan was slice off the section of the submarine containing the reactors and graft on a whole new unit containing replacement power plants. However, this was rejected on grounds of cost. Besides, '*The Little Golden Fish*' had already been superseded by more modern craft.

In 1982, fourteen years after the accident it was decided to dump her in the submarine graveyard in the nearby Kara Sea; ironically even this scuttling operation went badly wrong.

The site chosen for K-27's final resting place was only 33 metres (108 feet) deep. This was well below the 3,000 metres required by the International Atomic Energy Agency for redundant nuclear submarines. When the submarine sank, her nose hit the bottom first leaving her stern protruding out of the water. This necessitated a naval tug actually ramming the submarine's stern to puncture her ballast tanks so that she would sink.

There remains considerable concern in the international nuclear community about the safety of this and other rusting nuclear submarines lying on the bed of the Kara Sea. It is feared in some quarters that the radioactive material decaying in K-27 could reach a critical level and cause an uncontrolled chain reaction - effectively a nuclear explosion.

However, a joint Russian/Norwegian scientific expedition to the site in 2012 did not find excessive levels of radiation. Nevertheless, the Russian authorities are still planning to remove K-27 from the sea bed. This is so that the radioactive material on board can be safely removed and disposed of on dry land.

The problems in disposing of a redundant liquid metal cooled reactor are considerable. In the case of K-27, the uranium fuel, control rods and the lead and bismuth are all fused together making this an especially delicate and dangerous task.

The French Government agency responsible for nuclear energy has gone so far as to donate a specially designed device for this task. This will be performed in a specific dry dock at the Gremikha Submarine Base.

It seems that the Russian authorities have tended to blow hot and cold when it comes to raising submarine K-27. Which is a matter of considerable concern to the Bellona Foundation. Founded in Oslo in 1986, this international environmental NGO is a body which keeps a watching brief over environmental pollution with particular reference to Norway and the Russian Arctic.

'According to our information, the K-27 is the most dangerous of the dumped reactors,' Nils Bøhmer, Bellona's general director and nuclear physicist said. 'We welcome the lifting of this submarine provided it can be done in a safe way – the longer it's underwater, the worse will be its condition and the harder it will be to lift.' (*Source: Bellona article June 20th 2017 by Charles Digges*).

The latest plan was floated by the Krylov State Research Institute based in the Russian city of St Petersburg. Using a specially designed hybrid vessel which will be a cross between a floating dry dock and a catamaran, they plan to raise the submarine by 2022. With the Damocles Sword of a catastrophic nuclear explosion hanging over this whole Arctic Region, it is to be hoped this latest venture will finally bear fruit.

Decades of the Russian naval authorities dumping radioactive waste into the Kara Sea has left a massive legacy of which K-27 is only the tip of this lethal iceberg. At a seminar in Moscow in 2011 jointly hosted by Rosatom the Russian State nuclear corporation and Bellona the Russians finally admitted the scale of the problem.

They provided an alarming list detailing precisely what has been sunk in the Kara Sea over previous years. The details according to Bellona are as follows:

17,000 containers of radioactive waste, 19 ships containing radioactive waste, 14 nuclear reactors, including five that still contain spent nuclear fuel; 735 other pieces of radioactively contaminated heavy machinery and the K-27 nuclear submarine with its two reactors loaded with nuclear fuel. *(Source Bellona Org article Published on August 28th 2012 by Charles Digges).*

This is a frightening and deadly legacy that should concern the whole world and not just Russia.

Ghosts In The Machine?
Soviet Submarines K - 140 & K - 429
Sveredovinsk, Russian Arctic
27th - 28th August 1968
Nizhny Novgorod, Volga Federal District
1970

Precisely how and what happened on 27th and 28th August in 1968 at the Soviet Naval dockyard of Severodvinsk remain shrouded in mystery. What is known is that Yankee Class Submarine K-140 was in dock for repairs.

This submarine was fairly new, having been constructed the year before. She was the first of the class of Soviet submarines to carry thermonuclear weapons. The precise nature of the repairs is unknown.

On 27th August following upgrading work, the control rods were raised in one of the submarine's reactors. Presumably they were accidentally removed completely because the reactor suddenly showed a drastic increase in power generation, temperature and pressure.

On this occasion, the reactor was brought back under control without a significant release of radiation or injury to personnel. In addition to the incorrect removal of the control rods it was found that they had also been wrongly wired.

Two years later, a remarkably similar accident occurred aboard K-429, a brand new Charlie Class submarine. She was in dock at the Krasnoe Sormovo shipyard in Nizhny Novgorod on the Volga River a long way south of the Russian Arctic.

There was what was described as an 'uncontrolled start-up' of one of the vessel's reactors leading to a spontaneous chain reaction. This caused a dangerous fire and the release of a significant amount of radioactivity. Precise details of damage and injury are unknown.

It is difficult to know what to make of that 'uncontrolled start-up'. Did the reactor manage to fire up on its own? Or did one of the workers start the whole process by the careless removal of control rods? No doubt the answer is buried somewhere in the files of the Russian military.

Submarine K-116
Coolant Leak from Reactor
2nd July 1979

On 2nd July 1979 Soviet submarine K-116 (NATO Class Echo 2) experienced an accident that was all too common in the Russian Navy. Whilst operating in the Bay of Vladimir in the Sea of Japan, coolant leaked from the reactor core of her port reactor causing radiation to spread throughout the vessel. Whilst an unspecified number of her crew received dangerously high levels of radiation there were, mercifully, no reported fatalities on this occasion. Whether or not any of the casualties died prematurely because of their irradiation is not known.

Between 1972 and 1982, a further three Soviet submarines had serious reactor accidents involving coolant and subsequent radiation leaks but with no reported casualties.

Submarine K431
Refuelling Accident
Chazhma Bay, Vladivostok, Russian Far East
10th August 1985

For her first twenty years Soviet Submarine K-431 had a trouble free service record. She was commissioned on 30th September 1965 and powered by two pressurised water reactors. Then on 10th August 1985, K-431's service life ended in the most catastrophic way possible.

To understand what happened next it is important to appreciate the role control rods play in maintaining the safe operation of a nuclear reactor. These rods are usually made of a combination of metals such as cadmium, boron and silver. This is because they can absorb the neutrons produced by a chain reaction.

By inserting them into the reactor they can either slow or completely stop the chain reaction from taking place by the absorption of neutrons. In other words they are the safety brake in the nuclear energy process. Their sudden removal from the reactor can lead to an uncontrolled nuclear reaction with catastrophic consequences.

This is exactly what happened to K-431 on that fateful summer's day in 1985. At the time, she was being refuelled in the submarine naval base of Chazhma Bay near Vladivostok in the Russian Far East. It was a delicate operation requiring a high level of precision from both equipment and its operatives.

Whilst the actual refuelling went according to plan, the reactor tank lid was replaced incorrectly and had to be lifted again. Unfortunately, the control mechanism ensuring the lid was lifted to a safe height was incorrectly positioned. As a result, the lid with the reactor control rods attached was hoisted too far. The complete removal of the rods from the reactor sparked an uncontrolled chain reaction leading to a massive explosion killing eight naval officers and two enlisted men.

The subsequent release of radioactive gas and particles irradiated 49 other personnel ten of whom suffered acute radiation sickness. Some of these were firemen called in to fight the blaze which raged for four hours after the explosion.

Fortunately, the high level of radiation that affected an area about 6 kilometres around the base had a short life and decayed after a few days. Nevertheless, this remains a serious nuclear tragedy that claimed and blighted a significant number of lives.

After the accident the severely damaged Submarine K-431 made one last voyage. She was towed to a berth at nearby Pavlovsk Bay where she remains quietly rusting away.

Chapter 14
Missile Silo Explosion
Titan Missile Disaster, Damascus, Arkansas
September 18th 1980

During the Cold War, the U.S. missile defence system presented an awesome display of nuclear power. Ranged across the breadth of the United States huge Titan ICBM missiles armed with nuclear bombs many times more powerful than those dropped on Hiroshima and Nagasaki waited in silos to be launched at a moments notice. To prevent an accidental launch of any of these missiles, many sophisticated fail safe devices were put in place. After all, nobody wanted to go to war with Russia by mistake!

Despite all these precautions, there was always the chance of a rogue accident spelling catastrophe. On Thursday September 18th 1980, just such an accident happened and it came close to devastating the state of Arkansas. The incident began innocently enough. Two technicians from the Propellant Transfer Systems Team were performing a routine check on the pressure of the oxidiser tank on a Titan 2 missile. The rocket was armed with a W-53 nuclear warhead. The missile was situated in a silo complex in Van Buren County in the heart of rural Arkansas.

The oxidiser tank in question was at the very top of the missile and the technicians were using a ratchet wrench for the check. Suddenly, the socket for the oxidiser tank fell off the ratchet. Dropping eighty feet it bounced off the silo structure and hit the side of the missile, piercing its fuel tank. The rocket's Aerozine 50 liquid fuel immediately began to pour out of the hole torn in the side of the rocket.

After the two PTS technicians and the team of missile operatives had evacuated the launch pad area, the emergency response teams arrived. By this time it was early the next morning. First into the silo were two investigators from the Propellant Transfer Systems Team to find out exactly what had been damaged. Their detection systems soon picked up the presence of an explosive atmosphere within the silo and they were ordered to evacuate. However, someone had to switch on the exhaust fan in the silo to help clear the volatile gases that had built up.

The only option was to order the team back in. One of the team Senior Airman David Livingston then re-entered the silo. Almost immediately the leaked fuel ignited in an enormous explosion. It was thought this was caused by the exhaust fan electrically arcing, probably as it was switched on by Livingston.

The force of the blast blew the 740 ton silo door and the second stage of the Titan missile well clear of the silo. Fuel in what remained of the missile then ignited throwing the nuclear warhead a further hundred feet from the launch complex.

The disaster cost David Livingston his life and injured twenty one other workers including his PTS colleague Sergeant Jeff Kennedy who survived. The extensive damage to the silo complex put it beyond repair and it was buried along with much of the debris from the blast. Fortunately, the safety devices on the warhead prevented a nuclear explosion or the escape of any radioactive material.

The nine megaton warhead was removed on a flatbed trailer a couple of days after the accident and taken to Little Rock Air Force Base sixty miles away. According to press reports, in spite of the severity of the explosion, the warhead was only slightly dented.

Today, over forty years after the Titan accident happened, there is little or no trace of its silo and launchpad. It now lies within an area of private land just over three miles from the little town of Damascus, Arkansas.

Like so much else attached to the Cold War and its nuclear balance of terror, this incident has faded from the collective memory. However, at a cost of millions of dollars it must still hold the record for being one of the most expensive dropped tool accidents in history.

Sources

Command and Control: Nuclear Weapons, the Damascus Accident, and the Illusion of Safety. Penguin Press. Eric Schlosser 2013

"Missile silo blast kills 1, hurts 21; no radiation leak" St. Petersburg Times. (Florida). AP, UPI. September 20, 1980.

"Air Force truck removes damaged warhead" Eugene - Register September 22nd 1980

Mark 6 Titan II Missile in silo similar to the ICBM
that was destroyed in the Arkansas accident
Photograph: US Department of Defense

Chapter 15
A Deadly Burial Ground
Andreeva Bay, Kola Peninsula, Russian Arctic
February 1982

Andreeva Bay lies on the far western coast of the Kola Peninsula in the Russian Arctic. For the last eighty years it has been the location of a number of bases for the Russian Navy. The original base was actually built in 1939 for German ships under the Hitler-Ribbentrop Pact; with the German declaration of war on Russia and conquest of Norway it became redundant and sank into obscurity.

After the Second World War and with the frosting of relations between East and West during the Cold War, Andreeva Bay took on a new strategic importance for the Soviets. A series of bases were constructed for the ships and submarines of the Soviet Northern Fleet. From 1961, one of them, known simply as 569 became a graveyard for redundant nuclear submarines and their radioactive waste.

By the 1980s, it was home to a hundred rusting submarine hulks and the deadly radioactive fuel waste still in their reactors. Since it was only thirty-four miles from the Norwegian border, there was considerable concern about the safety and stability of so much decaying radioactive waste on the West's doorstep. Fears were expressed that so much unstable and dangerous material could possibly ignite creating a huge nuclear explosion. The dump was also only thirty-seven miles from the large Russian city of Murmansk.

In February 1982, an incident occurred that seemed to bear out these fears of a nuclear catastrophe. Building Number 5 was a repository for a large amount of nuclear waste contained in drums; 4000 of these drums each containing 350 kilograms of waste were suspended by large chains in two pools of water measuring 200 foot long by 10 foot wide. The drums were kept apart to prevent the decaying radioactive waste from accidentally combining into a critical mass and triggering an uncontrollable chain reaction.

By the 1980s, Building 5 was already in a state of advanced dilapidation with faulty electoral equipment and numerous holes in its roof. Many of the drums containing the nuclear waste had also broken loose from the chains holding them. Sinking to the bed of the pool, they piled up haphazardly one on top of the other. This led to the real threat of the waste reaching that critical mass and subsequent nuclear explosion. It was, in fact, a major nuclear accident waiting to happen and happen it did. In February 1982, the metal coating on the concrete of the right hand pool failed causing it to leak 700,000 tons of highly radioactive water into the Barents Sea over the next two years.

On discovering the leak the base managers ordered 20 sacks of flour to be poured into the pool hoping that the dough this created would seal the cracks causing the leak. This did not work. In April 1982, 600 cubic metres of concrete were poured into the tank to stem the continuing outflow of radioactive water. This also proved to be ineffective. By October of that year, the leakage was reaching dangerous levels threatening to irradiate not just the whole base area but also the surrounding marine environment.

In desperation, it was decided to cover the whole storage area with concrete containing lead and iron in place of conventional stone aggregates. This seemed to do the trick and by November 1982 the leakage of radioactive water had been drastically reduced. There were a number of theories as to why the leaks occurred in the metal sheathed concrete walls and base of the pool.

Experts finally concluded that the most likely explanation lay in the original design of pools. When they were constructed, it was assumed that the heat from the decaying nuclear waste would be sufficient to protect them from the temperature extremes of the arctic environment. In other words, this built-in heat source would keep the water at a constant temperature preventing excessive expansion and contraction from the freezing arctic winters tearing the pools apart.

Working on this hypothesis, the designers decided it was unnecessary to include an additional heating plant for the water. They were wrong and the surface of the water froze over to depth of approximately eight inches in the extreme arctic winters. The subsequent unplanned expansion of the water caused structural failure in the pool walls and the welds in the protective metal sheathing.

In an attempt to resolve this problem a crude and unorthodox solution was decided upon that was strictly in breach of international radiation safety standards. A hole was smashed in the ice covering the water in the pool and a pipe connected to a boiler was inserted into the water beneath. Steam was then pumped in to melt the surface ice. Whilst this worked it also caused radioactive steam from the melted ice to spread throughout Building Number 5 and the surrounding environment. Whether this caused any injuries or fatalities remains unknown.

In February 1983, building Number 5 was closed with no more

waste being stored there. Plans were also put in place to remove all the existing drums of nuclear materials in the two storage pools. Unfortunately, this was done with little regard to the safety and wellbeing of the workers.

In 1983, the Soviet authorities embarked upon a drastic course of action to remove the nuclear threat from Building Number 5. Every two or three months a four carriage freight train would leave Andreeva Base to make a 3000 kilometre journey south to the Urals.

Hidden behind the green panelling in the rail trucks were containers of the spent nuclear waste from Building Number 5. The destination of these trains was Mayak, the most secret of all nuclear facilities being the birthplace of the Soviet H-bomb (*See Chapter 4*). Six years later on 13th December 1989 the last train arrived at Mayak in the Urals. All but 25 drums of the unstable, toxic nuclear waste had been removed from Building 5, Andreeva Bay. Those remaining drums had proved impossible to extract.

Not only had the extraction been very long, it had also proved to be highly dangerous. On one occasion a poorly protected worker fell into the radioactive water covering the nuclear waste. With no regard for his own safety, a fellow worker called Semenov jumped in and pulled the other man to safety. They had both received high levels of radiation and it is not recorded whether they ultimately survived.

There have also been many anecdotal reports by workers of mini chain reactions caused by nuclear waste spilling from the containers as they were extracted from building Number 5.

A.F. Safonov leader of the clean-up gave a vivid account of of this in his book *In death's embrace under radioactive water at the Andreeva Bay*:

'This phenomenon was observed by nearby sailors. Of course, we did not file any official reports. The navy usually concealed such information to avoid taking the blame…

' *Blue-green flashes of light were also observed in the left-hand pool in building #5 during the work on lifting nuclear waste drums from the bottom. That they were uncontrolled chain reactions was confirmed by the physicist, senior lieutenant Leonid Grigorievich Konobritski, who served then in building #5.'*

Safonov's descriptions of these chain reactions with their 'blue-green flashes of light' are typical of criticality accidents described in Chapter 6.

Whilst the immediate threat from Building No 5 has been solved by removing the waste elsewhere, the deadly legacy of Andreeva Bay remains. According to Charles Digges of Bellona, in 2017, 22,000 nuclear fuel units remained under the chilly arctic waters of Andreeva Bay. The potential of some form of catastrophic accident contaminating the surrounding seas was of particular concern to Norway whose border lay in such close proximity to the Russian base.

Fortunately, even the highly secret echelons of the Russian nuclear and military establishment have not proved to be totally immune to international pressure. In 1994, Bellona the Norwegian Foundation dedicated to highlighting environmental threats such as the Andreeva nuclear waste danger, opened an office in Murmansk. Predictably, their investigations into the nuclear waste dump at Andreeva sparked a hostile response.

In February 1996, Bellona's Russian expert Alexander Nikitin, a former Soviet naval officer, was charged with treason by espionage by the FSB (The KGB's successor) for his contributions to Bellona's report on the nuclear safety within the Russian Northern Fleet.[3] *He was fully acquitted by the Russian Supreme Court in 2000.*

This may have been due to the pressure from the Norwegian Government who were very concerned by the the nuclear waste threat to their adjacent coastline. It seems this strong diplomatic pressure by the Norwegian Government on their Russian counterparts had finally begun to bear fruit.

Fortunately, the grim reality of the contamination threat from the Andreeva nuclear waste finally overrode the geopolitical differences between Russia and her neighbours. From 1996 to 2017 Norway and Russia co-operated in a massive clean-up of the Andreeva Bay site. Norway alone contributed 30 million euros to this project. Throughout that period UK, France, Germany and Italy also provided logistical support.

An indication of what a big job this clean-up has been is that the first consignment of waste only left Andreeva Bay in the summer of 2017. In June of that year, that first consignment of nuclear waste was transported from Andreeva to Murmansk on the cargo ship *Rossita*. From there it was transported in special trains to Mayak near Chelyabinsk in the Urals.

To underline the symbolic importance of that event, Berge Brende, the Norwegian Foreign Minister headed up a delegation from his country to see the consignment off.

Safety concerns about the waste have not entirely gone away. The waste train has to travel a huge distance through many populated areas before reaching its final destination at Mayak. No matter how good security and safety is on that journey, the possibility of an accident is always there.

There is also the question of how safe the recycling and disposal of the waste will be at Mayak. Conditions at the plant have undoubtedly improved since the 1950s, but Norway and Russia's other partners have to rely on her to ensure that utmost safety and security is observed at the plant.

Low resolution photograph of Andreeva Bay showing submarines possibly awaiting disposal.
Photograph courtesy Lelique/Russian Wikipedia

Sources

Bellona Foundation, Vulkan 11, 0178 Oslo, Norway. www.bellona.org

Chapter 16
A Classic Case of Human Error
Donen Nuclear Plant, Tokaimura, Japan
11th March 1997 & 30th September 1999

The Tokai Nuclear Power Plant was originally established in the early 1960s close to the village of Tokai about half way down the coast of Japan and 110 kilometres from Tokyo. It was Japan's first nuclear plant producing electricity from 1966 until decommissioning in 1998.

A second plant was built in the 1970s and produced electricity until it was shut down as a result of the Tōhoku earthquake and tsunami in 2011. This was the most powerful earthquake in Japan's history and was the cause of the Fukushima Nuclear Plant disaster. Until then, neither Tokai plant experienced any serious incidents in their working lives.

Adjoining the 180 acre complex that houses these two redundant plants is a smaller experimental plant run by the Donen Company (Power Reactor and Nuclear Fuel Development Corporation (PNC). This plant also reprocesses nuclear fuels.

In the evening of Tuesday 11th March 1997, there was a small explosion in the reprocessing plant. Although the explosion caused limited damage it did release quite a serious amount of radiation. Thirty-seven workers were subjected to elevated levels of radiation. A week after the explosion, a significant spike in the levels of radioactive caesium isotopes was recorded twenty-five miles down the coast.

The cause of the explosion was the mixing of reprocessed liquid nuclear waste with bitumen in a drum to solidify and stabilise it. However, a fire broke out during this volatile process which was extinguished. The drum and its contents were left to cool down.

Unfortunately the extinguishing process proved inadequate and instead of cooling down, the radioactive bitumen mixture continued to smoulder until it exploded twenty hours later. Providentially, this incident, though potentially serious did not leave any lasting damage to humans or the surrounding environment. Two years later, another incident occurred that would have much more serious consequences.

On 30th September 1999 three workers at the Donen plant were preparing a batch of fuel for the plant's experimental fast breeder reactor known as *Joyo*. It was was the first time in three years this had been done. It appears none of the three operatives involved in this had received any specialist training to perform this delicate task.

The fuel they were going to feed to the reactor was a solution of highly radioactive uranium known as uranyl nitrate. Because of its extremely volatile nature, the correct procedure for adding this to the reactor was via a buffer tank. Having been placed in a buffer tank, the fuel should have been pumped gently into the reactor's precipitation tank at quantities of 2.5 kg at a time.

For some inexplicable reason, the three workers decided to by-pass this procedure. Instead they poured the uranyl nitrate directly into the reactor's precipitation tank from a stainless steel bucket. This solution also contained thirty-five pounds of uranium which took the total amount in the precipitation tank over the safety limit where a simultaneous chain reaction would start. What followed was a classic criticality accident.

This occurred in short order with a blue flash triggering radiation leak alarms. Two of the workers immediately received what would prove to be fatal doses of radiation. They were Hisashi Ouchi whose body was actually draped over the precipitation tank and his colleague Masato Shinohara who was standing on a platform with the bucket of the uranyl nitrate fuel.

Both men suffered acute pain and nausea as they staggered through to the decontamination room helped by their colleague Yutaka Yokokawa. He had been sitting at a desk four metres from the reactor. That distance from the explosion probably saved his life. Whilst in the room Ouchi began vomiting before rapidly losing consciousness.

The chain reaction continued until the next day before it was finally brought under control. During that time, large amounts of radioactive particles leaked from the reactor contaminating the plant and the surrounding area. A total of 667 emergency workers, plant workers and residents were exposed to excess radiation. Many of these had to be hospitalised for treatment.

Both Ouchi and Shinohara received doses of radiation that ultimately proved unsurvivable. Ouchi died on 21st December 1999 whilst Shinohara's damaged immune system was unable to fight off infection and he passed away in the following April. Yokokawa survived by dint of the fact that was sitting far enough away from the incident to receive a much lower dose of radiation.

The International Atomic Energy Agency ruled that the accident was caused by 'human error and serious breaches of safety principles.' JCO, the company that owned the Donen plant had to pay $121 million to settle 6,875 claims to people exposed to the leaked radiation.

Six JCO employees including the plant administrator and Yutaka Yokokawa the sole survivor of the accident pleaded guilty to negligence causing death, in court proceedings held in April 2001.

However, before we race too hastily to judge those six people for this accident, there is an important fact that should be borne in mind. In 1995 a safety committee in Donen had approved the use of stainless steel buckets in the process of manufacturing the radioactive fuel for the reactor. Moreover this process had been recommended in an unauthorised company manual since 1996.

Apart from Fukushima, the Tokaimura criticality accident remains the worst civilian radiation accident in Japanese history. It is registered at Level 4 on the INES scale of nuclear disasters.

Sources

World Nuclear Association www.world-nuclear.org

The Tokaimura Incident - Paper by Anthony Brown, Stanford University 24th February 2015

"Nuclear Workers Appeared Unaware of Dangers". Los Angeles Times. 7 October 1999

Chapter 17
The Kitty Litter Nuclear Explosion
Waste Isolation Pilot Plant, Carlsbad, New Mexico
14th February 2014

The safe and permanent disposal of radioactive waste has been the Holy Grail for the nuclear industry since the beginning of the atomic age. With much of this waste material having a half life of many thousands of years, it is imperative that a waste storage facility has to be deep and remote enough to put used radioactive material beyond reach of anyone with ill intent wishing to steal it. In some cases of course, like Mayak in the Urals, Andreeva Bay in the Arctic and Rocky Flats in Colorado, safe disposal was completely ignored with dire results.

With this in mind, The United States Atomic Energy Commission (Now known as the Department of Energy) began the search for a suitable underground storage facility. The first site at Lyons in the state of Kansas was rejected due to strong opposition from the local populace and the discovery of oil and gas reserves in the area. These were thought to compromise the safety of the storage facility.

The second site the AEC chose was in a sparsely populated area of New Mexico. Fortunately, the local population, mainly in the town of Carlsbad approximately twenty miles from the proposed site did not object to it. Another important reason for choosing this site was because it consisted in a large part of a 3,000 foot thick ancient salt deposit half a mile underground. This was known as the Delaware Basin. The facility would be known as The Waste Isolation Pilot Plant (WIPP).

Burying nuclear waste deep in such salt rock deposits was considered to be the safest option since they contained no running water sources that could be contaminated by the radioactive waste. These salt deposits also naturally seal all fractures and openings to form a further thick protective layer over the buried waste. This is known as 'salt creep' in the salt mining industry.

The WIPP took over twenty years of construction and testing and cost $1 billion dollars. It would take only waste products of the U.S. nuclear weapons industry. Drilling shafts and the creation of subterranean storage areas began in 1975. On March 26th 1999, the WIPP took its first delivery of radioactive waste from Los Alamos. The original plan was that when the subterranean caverns are completely filled with drums of waste between 2025 and 2035, they will be collapsed and then covered by thirteen layers of concrete. The estimated total cost of the project is $19 billion dollars.

For its first fifteen years the plant operated without incident. Then on 14th February 2014 one of the barrels of radioactive waste suddenly exploded spreading radiation throughout the otherwise pristine environment. Some radiation also escaped into the wider atmosphere contaminating seventeen workers above ground.

After an extensive investigation, the authorities finally nailed down the cause of this unexpected explosion. Before being transported from the Los Alamos Laboratories to the WIPP, the plutonium and americium waste was packed with cat litter in 55 gallon drums. This litter had been found to be an ideal material for soaking up and stabilising radioactive waste particularly in semi-liquid form. On this occasion, the operatives made the crucial error of using organic litter rather than the inert, clay based alternative.

It is thought that one of the chemical components of the litter reacted with the waste causing the explosion. What seemed to be a small mistake had extensive ramifications. The WIPP was immediately closed and there were murmurs that it might never reopen. Other barrels of radiological waste in other storage facilities were also found to contain organic cat litter.

The cost of this accident had been estimated to be as high as $2 billion. This would have made it the most expensive nuclear accident in U.S. history. However, the plant reopened in 2017 after a clean up at a total cost of $500 million. Whilst only a quarter of the earlier frightening estimate, it was hardly peanuts.

The Waste Isolation Pilot Plant near Carlsbad, New Mexico.
Photograph Courtesy Leaflet Own Work Public Domain/Wikimedia

Footnote
Signs of the Times

The purpose of WIPP and other underground nuclear burial sites is to put such waste permanently beyond reach. Which has raised another interesting problem for the nuclear industry. Permanent disposal means this waste will be buried for as long as it is dangerously radioactive. In the case of materials such as plutonium this will be as much as 240,000 years.

By that time human culture will have evolved beyond recognition presumably with totally different languages and methods of communication. Since 1983, the Department of Energy has been working on a form of communication to warn future humans of the deadly danger of this radiological waste. In doing this, they have cast their net wide enlisting the help of specialists ranging from archaeologists to linguists and even science fiction writers.

In the case of WIPP, it is proposed that 32 twenty-five foot high granite pillars will be erected in a four square mile area surrounding the subterranean storage site. Within this latter day Stonehenge will be a massive 33 foot high earth barrier which will be 100 feet wide.

Just for good measure, sixteen more granite columns will be placed within this wall. Within this there will be a roofless building directly above the burial site. It will contain warning information about the site in the six official languages of the United Nations: English, Spanish, Russian, French, Chinese and Arabic. There will also be inscriptions in Navajo Indian. To allow for future linguistic developments, ample space will be left for future translations. In addition there will also be visual signs such as a figure running from a skull and a radiation symbol.

It would indeed be fascinating to see what our distant descendants will make of all this. Let us hope it does not kill them.

One of the image only signs considered for use at the WIPP to warn citizens of the far future away from the radioactive waste storage area.

Chapter 18
A Mysterious Blast in The White Sea
Nyonoksa, Archangelsk Oblast, Russian Federation
8th August 2019

What happened in The White Sea in Arctic Russia on 8th August 2019 has all the hallmarks of a spy thriller. The story comes complete with the destruction of a revolutionary new weapon, false trails and a mysterious ending.

Nyonoksa is a typical Russian rural village of wooden houses and a traditional church with onion domes. It nestles on the banks of the Dvina River that flows into the White Sea in the Russian Arctic. Unlike thousands of other such settlements, Nyonoksa has a top secret military base on its doorstep.

Known as the State Central Navy Testing Range, it is used to test experimental weapons such as cruise missiles for the Russian Navy. The range is presumably situated on the coast so that any missiles that went awry would plunge into The White Sea rather than endanger the settlements of this sparsely populated region.

However, this did not prevent a rogue missile threatening Nyonoksa in December 2015. On that occasion a missile exploded on take off sending debris flying in all directions. One part of the rocket hit a wooden block of flats in the village setting it ablaze. Miraculously nobody seems to have been hurt in that incident.

By the summer of 2017, the Russian Military had been working hard on developing a revolutionary new cruise missile. Known as *9M730 Burevestnik*, it is a nuclear powered cruise missile with unlimited range and an ability to evade enemy radar. *Burevestnik* is the Russian word for petrel or storm bringer which seems to be an appropriate name for such a fearsome weapon.

What makes this cruise missile a game changer is that, unlike its western counterparts, it does not rely on liquid fuel propellant which limits the range of all these weapons. Instead, it is powered by a miniature nuclear reactor that can effectively allow *The Petrel* to fly indefinitely.

Since it is a cruise missile, it can fly close to the ground and under any radar that would pick up high altitude Inter Continental Ballistic Missiles.

One major problem with a nuclear powered cruise missile is that its exhaust would leave a trail of harmful radioactive isotopes across the territory it flies over. Yes, this would do additional harm to an adversary but it would also harm friendly forces as well. Also, development of such small nuclear plants is a tricky business.

According to U.S. intelligence sources, the development of *The Petrel* (NATO codename: *Skyfall*) has been dogged by problems with three out of four launches failing. The Russians deny this, insisting the development of the missile has so far been successful. It would be surprising if the development of a new weapon did not involve some accidents. Western intelligence sources place the number of failed launches of *Petrel* since 2016 as high as sixteen.

These earlier launches had been carried out at a number of test sites such as Kapustin Yar in Russian Central Asia and Pankovo, Northern Russia. These had all been closely monitored by U.S. spy satellites. It seems the next set of tests on the missile would be carried out at the Nyonoksa site which was more remote and less open to scrutiny.

Nevertheless, there were still plenty of electrical monitoring sites in the area listening in to what was happening at the missile range for total secrecy to be maintained. On 8th August 2019 sensors at monitoring stations in the neighbourhood of Nyonoksa and as far away as Norway picked up a major seismic event at six a.m. Shortly after that, radiation sensoring equipment at local monitoring stations registered a brief sharp spike in radiation levels. Some sources have estimated that the spike was 40 times the normal level of radiation.

At the same time a group of fisherman in the White Sea allegedly witnessed a Soviet navy salvage vessel enveloped in a 300 foot column of white water from what appeared to be a massive explosion. One of the fisherman would later report that the ship was severely damaged with a large hole in her side.

It was obvious that something fairly catastrophic had happened but what? The official Russian version was that an accident had occurred as a result of a failed test of an 'isotope power source for a liquid-fuelled rocket engine.' Isotope power source is another way of saying nuclear power plant indicating it was probably the engine of a *Burevestnik* cruise missile that exploded. One might query why conventional fuel was mentioned for a nuclear powered rocket. In fact the *Burevestnik* has a conventionally fuelled ramjet engine presumably to aid take off and achieve maximum cruise speed.

What appears to have happened is that a *Burevestnik* launch at Nyonoksa failed causing the missile to crash and sink in the White Sea.

During the subsequent recovery operation on that fateful August morning, something drastic seems to have gone wrong causing a nuclear reaction in the missile being recovered. This ignited the volatile liquid fuel in the missile leading to a massive explosion severely damaging the salvage vessel.

At least six workers on this vessel were rushed to the the nearby city of Archangel suffering from high doses of radiation. Once there, three of the victims were treated at the Semashko Medical Centre which was equipped to deal with victims of radiation accidents. The other three were sent to the Archangel Regional Clinical Hospital which had no proper facilities to deal with radiation accidents. Worse, none of the staff at the hospital were warned they would have to treat patients with high levels of radiation. Unlike the Semashko Medical Centre, the regional clinical hospital had no hazmat suits or other protective clothing. As a result of their exposure to highly radioactive patients, all the staff and doctors at the Regional Clinical Hospital were medevaced to the Burnazyan Federal and Biophysical Centre in Moscow. This was alongside the six severely ill victims who had been injured in the blast. According to one unnamed medical worker two of those died of radiation sickness before reaching Moscow. Back in Archangel, all the rooms in the Regional Clinical Hospital where the victims had been treated were sealed off and deep cleaned.

Although the Russian Authorities initially admitted that two personnel had been killed in the Nyonoksa accident, they later increased the death toll to five. On 12th August 2019, in the main square of Sarov, the city which includes the Russian Federation Nuclear Centre, there was a viewing of the five coffins of the dead. On 12th November 2019 they were all posthumously awarded The Order of Courage. It also emerged that they were all high ranking nuclear scientists. Their loss must have been a grievous blow to the Russian nuclear establishment as well as a terrible tragedy for the families involved.

Meanwhile, reports of the disaster were filtering out via the World's media. On 9th August, the BBC online website carried a story about the explosion under the headline: "Five Confirmed Dead in Rocket Blast."

The article stated that Rosatom, the Russian state nuclear corporation which works closely with the Russian military, had lost five of their employees in the explosion not two as previously stated by the authorities. It also quoted a Rosatom source that the dead were all working on a liquid propellant fuel engine.

The BBC also reported that there had been a 40 minute spike in radiation levels shortly after the explosion around the neighbouring city of Severodvinsk. This, in turn had caused panic buying of iodine as an antidote to radiation poisoning. A similar buying rush of iodine occurred after the Chernobyl accident. This is because iodine or potassium iodide can help to block the thyroid gland from being attacked by radiation.

The authorities later deleted all mention of the radioactive spike from their online outlets. When asked by the BBC why, they gave this illuminating reply: "Because this incident comes under the authority of the Defence Ministry".

For its part, the Russian Defence Ministry insisted that 'there have been no harmful chemicals released into the atmosphere, the radiation levels are normal.'

Whilst Russian Government sources desperately tried to downplay the accident, reports continued to filter out through international media. On 10th August, two days after the accident Voice of America online posted a report with the questioning headline: 'What exactly happened at Russian Missile Test Site?' In it, the report relayed information from Archangel regional news site 29.ru that all the pharmacies in the city had sold out of iodine. It also reported that there was a month long ban on fishing and swimming in The White Sea.

On 28th August 2019, the Australian website news.au.com carried a Reuters interview with Anne Stroemmen Lycke the chief executive of Norsar, the Norwegian nuclear Treaty monitoring agency. In it she stated:

'We registered two explosions, of which the last one coincided in time with the reported increase in radiation, both blasts were registered on our infrasound system. The first was also picked up by seismology.'

This could indicate a missile first crashing on launch and then its nuclear power plant exploding as it was being salvaged.

On 30th August 2019 the independent *Moscow Times* online newspaper gave what was probably the fullest accounts of the disaster so far. Under the headline '*Russia's Mystery Nuclear Explosion Occurred During Missile Recovery at Sea*' it reported that *The mysterious explosion in northern Russia that caused a spike in radiation levels happened during a mission to salvage a nuclear-powered cruise missile from the bottom of the sea.*

Five nuclear engineers were killed in a liquid propulsion system blast at Russia's naval missile test facility, leading to a brief spike in radiation on Aug. 8. The secrecy surrounding the accident has led outside observers to speculate that what the explosion involved was the Burevestnik nuclear-powered intercontinental cruise missile, dubbed the SSC-X-9 Skyfall by NATO.

In early September 2019 two pontoons loaded with what appeared to be damaged metal parts were washed up on a beach 2.5 miles from Nyonoksa. Radioactive readings taken close to the pontoons by the Belomorkanal news site indicated they were highly radioactive. Markings on the side of the pontoons indicated they were from the site of the explosion.

Strangely, although the two vessels were dangerously radioactive, the authorities failed to post any guards or establish any security fencing on the beach where the pontoons had landed up. Not that local people seemed to be in any hurry to approach them. One Nyonoksa resident posted a photograph of the two pontoons on social media with the caption: *'This is what death looks like.'*

As in Soviet times, the Russians remain very secretive about all but the basic details of the accident. This has led to a huge amount of speculation and confusion surrounding the event. There is even disagreement amongst western nuclear specialists about the cause of the explosion. On the one side Jeffrey Lewis and Federation of American Scientists fellow Ankit Panda think the explosion was most likely caused by a test of the *Burevestnik* cruise missile. On the other hand Ian Williams of the Center for Strategic and International Studies and James Acton of the Carnegie Endowment for International Peace did not think the Russians had enough financial and technical resources to develop such a cruise missile. I have to say, in the face of all the intelligence information indicating multiple launches of the *Burevestnik* since 2016, the latter seems an odd conclusion.

At the time of writing, what happened at The Nyonoksa Range in August 2019 remains unclear except that five people died as a result of a large explosion. I believe that the account I have given here which I gleaned from many sources is probably closest to the truth. This could change when all the facts finally emerge as they undoubtedly will. The truth will out as the old adage goes.

Footnote
The Long History of Cruise Missiles

Like much of the military technology covered in this book, cruise missiles have their beginnings over seventy years ago in the Second World War. The father of these weapons was the German V1 Flying Bomb which bears a striking resemblance to its modern day descendants. Whilst its technology is crude by today's standards, the VI 'Doodlebug' was a formidable and terrifying weapon for the wartime British population to face. Once again we must be thankful that its introduction came too late to change the course of the War.

The *Burevestnik* missile covered earlier in this chapter may seem revolutionary with its nuclear powered engine, but in fact even this is comparatively old technology. Way back in 1956, the U.S. Government began developing just such a weapon. Called The Supersonic Low Altitude Missile or SLAM it was an unmanned aerial vehicle designed to deliver nuclear bombs to enemy targets at supersonic speeds.

It was a truly radical aircraft for its time with a nuclear powered ramjet engine giving it a range of 113,000 miles (182,000 km) and a cruising speed of 3,222 mph. With such a range, SLAM could cruise the world at high altitudes for long periods of time before dropping to near ground level to deliver its deadly payload.

SLAM's nuclear power plants were also revolutionary measuring only 57.25 inches (1.454 m) by 64.24 inches (1.632 m) long. To withstand the stresses of extreme temperature and speed these nuclear power plants were constructed using special high grade ceramics.

The fuel rods for the reactor were equally tiny being hollow hexagonal tubes about 4 inches (10 cm) long with an inside diameter of 0.227 inches (5.8 mm). Made from a refractory ceramic base, these elements were designed to operate at a temperature of 2,330 °F (1,277 °C).

In May 1961 Tory-IIA, the first of these nuclear powered engines was successfully tested on a dedicated proving range at Jackass Flats in the Nevada Desert. Whilst that particular test lasted only a few seconds, three years later, its successor engine, Tory IIC ran on full power for five minutes.

These preliminary trials were performed on test beds. What was needed now was an airframe to put the engines in and only then would the SLAM project be close to completion. However, no missile framework had yet been constructed to take the engines. At that stage the world's first cruise missile was still on the drawing board and that was where it was destined to stay.

In the summer of 1964, the Pentagon who were sponsoring the whole project suddenly took fright. In the eyes of the top brass, the rising costs of developing SLAM did not compare well with Intercontinental Missiles. It seemed they could deliver their bombs to Moscow much quicker and cheaper than this half missile/half plane.

Other more political considerations also came into play. Siren voices could be heard saying that the whole idea was 'too provocative' and could force the Soviets into developing similar weapons. Where would we be then? In another unwanted arms race that's where! Inevitably, on 1st July 1964, the military finally pulled the plug on SLAM, the cruise missile that never was.

Ironically, forty years later, the new generation of cruise missiles have proved their worth time and again in recent wars. As for those ICBMs, they are now looking very much like relics of the past.

Sources

Five Confirmed Dead in Rocket Blast. BBC Online 9/08/2019

What exactly happened at Russian Missile Test Site? VOA 10/08/2019

www.news.au.com 28/ 08/2019

Russia's Mystery Nuclear Explosion Occurred During Missile Recovery at Sea

Moscow Times 38/08/2019

www.military-today.com

*An Atmospheric Nuclear Ramjet: the Supersonic Low Altitude Missil*e Federico Rossi, Stanford University, March 17, 2016

SLAM/Pluto Project www.GlobalSecurity.com

The first cruise missile - German V1 “Doodlebug” flying bomb from the Second World War at RAF Manston History Museum.
Photograph by Nick Brazil

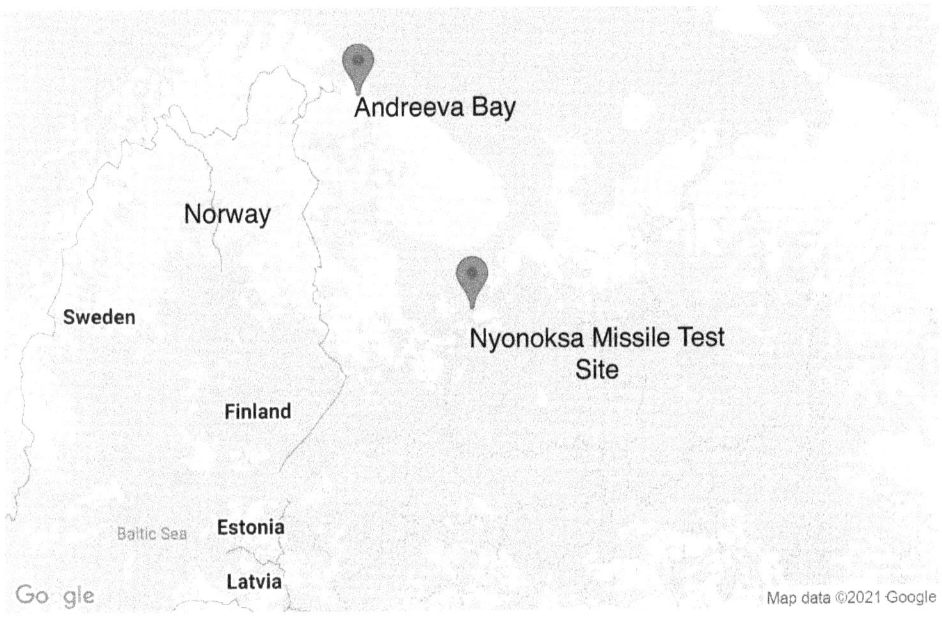

Map showing locations of Nyonoksa Missile Test Site and Andreeva Bay in the Russian Arctic where large quantities of radioactive waste has been dumped by the Russian Navy close to the Norwegian border

The *Burevestnik* 9M730 nuclear cruise missile is thought to closely resemble this Russian Kalibr conventionally powered cruise missile.

Image: Shutterstock

Artists impression of the Pluto/SLAM experimental cruise missile from the Ling-Temco-Vought consortium.
Image Courtesy GlobalSecurity.org

Chapter 19
The Nuclear Disaster Next Door
Tamara Schiopu's Story

Chişinău, the capital city of Moldova is 486 kilometres or 304 miles as the crow flies from Chernobyl in neighbouring Ukraine. At the time of the Chernobyl Disaster in April 1986, Tamara Schiopu was a young teacher living in Chişinău and about to get married. Whilst this book is about other nuclear accidents than Chernobyl, her personal impression of that catastrophic event has been included because it gives a valuable human perspective on all such tragedies.

Chernobyl and I

In April 1986 I was 21, just about to graduate from University and madly in love with my future (now-ex) husband. I was as carefree as any young girl can be in spring and the scarce news about Chernobyl that was coming through was sieving through my brain like water. I remember hearing someone saying on TV or radio that the world should not get so wired up about Chernobyl, because the Americans had much worse atomic accidents and nobody had judged them. So that was all right then…

That piece of information, about *'those Americans'* put my mind completely at rest, as I did not need to know anything else. I was as brainwashed as any normal person of my generation.

Occasionally we would hear from friends and neighbours 'that person got recruited to work at Chernobyl' and that the money they earned there was fantastic; I remember the sum mentioned – 3,000 roubles per month. To give you a comparison- my salary as a new teacher after university was going to be 106 roubles a month for 36 hours/week work.

So, the 3,000 rouble salary was something to dream about...

In fact we got married in August, everything was 'normal' and to make matters worse – I was really keen and got pregnant in November with my first baby. Nobody ever mentioned to me about the risks of having children under radiation, and of course – I had no idea of how high the radiation levels were in Moldova at that time.

This was a crime against future mothers and children – not warning them of the risks associated with radiation poisoning. And I continuously think how lucky I am and my son is to be normal and healthy. However I know that the cancer cells are deep down there and any day they might be triggered by something.... Of course, we will never know whether this would be directly linked to Chernobyl. The truth and fact is though, I was there, showered with high radiation, as was my baby, and what's to come we are yet to see.

Many years later, while living in England I met a young lady from my city Chişinău who told me the story of her own family. She was s small child when the disaster happened and her father got called in the middle of the night to work; he disappeared for three months. Whenever her mother tried to find out about his whereabouts at his workplace, she was told 'he is on a business trip, he is fine and will be back soon.' He returned after three months, told the family where he had been, but because of the lack of information, the family did not feel worried, at least the children did not learn the truth.

By Tamara Schiopu, Moldova

Map showing Chişinău, Moldova in relation to Chernobyl,Ukraine

Map created by Nick Brazil using Google Template

Chapter 20
In Conclusion
February 2021

The nuclear age has been with us now since 1942. During that time the number of countries possessing nuclear weapons has grown from two (the U.S. and the U.K.) in 1945 to about a dozen. In addition to them, there are plenty of other nations such as Iran who are keen to join their number.

The motivation for countries to possess these weapons of mass destruction is not so much to use them, but to give even a small nation political clout. The knowledge that to actually use their nuclear weapons in anger would spell a country's own destruction has invariably prevented even the most extreme dictator from hitting the button. The fact that both Pakistan and India have never used their nuclear weapons in their various wars is a good example of this.

Nevertheless, we live in an increasingly unstable and dangerous world. So, there is no guarantee that some of the 14,000 or so nuclear weapons scattered across the globe will not be used in war at some future date. At the time of writing (2021), The People's Republic of China is behaving in an increasingly belligerent manner. Whether it is in its attempted takeover of the South China Sea or massing troops along the Sino-Indian Border, the PRC is pushing its considerable power like never before.

Such activities are fraught with danger. Who is to say that if Communist China mounted a full-scale invasion of Northern India as they did in 1962, that the Indian Government would not hit the nuclear button as a last resort? There is also the continuing danger that one of the world's many terror groups could obtain a nuclear weapon and actually detonate it.

Apart from the poisoned chalice of nuclear weapons, there is also nuclear power for the provision of electricity. In December 2019 there were 30 countries operating 455 nuclear power plants with 54 under construction. In the case of France (70.6%), Slovakia (53.9%), Ukraine (53.9%), and Hungary (49.2%), nuclear power provides a significant percentage of their electricity.

At the other end of the scale is Italy closing all her nuclear power plants in 1990. This was done after the majority in a referendum voted for it in 1987. Then there is Austria and the Philippines who have never used their reactors since they were built. Germany, Belgium, Spain and

Switzerland are all planning to phase out nuclear power in favour of greener alternatives.

All six of Germany's plants are due to be shut down by 2022. This was very much a political reaction to the Fukushima disaster. At the time of writing nuclear provides 10.1% of Germany's electricity. It is an open question whether any green energy alternative can replace this loss of electrical power. There is a similar plan to shut down Belgium's seven plants that provide 47.6% of that country's electricity.

Replacement of nearly half of Belgium's electrical power provision presents an even bigger challenge than its German neighbour. No doubt Spain which relies on nuclear to provide 21.4% of her electricity and Switzerland at 23.9% will face similar dilemmas.

What is happening in those 'refusenik' countries like Germany and Belgium is the tip of the iceberg. Over the past few decades people have been turning away from nuclear power. The main reason is that thanks to four high profile accidents starting with Windscale in 1957 and ending with Three Mile Island in 1979, Chernobyl in 1986 and Fukushima in 2011 the nuclear industry has developed a reputation for being a highly dangerous energy source.

I feel this is undeserved and is based on many myths and misconceptions that have become regarded as unassailable truths over the years. In fact, nuclear power is probably one of the most misunderstood sources of energy creation. All too often it is regarded by those opposed to it as a deadly threat to human life and the environment. Accidents such as those described in this book and more famous incidents such as Chernobyl and Fukushima might also be used to reinforce this view.

This overlooks the fact that nuclear power is by far and away one of the safest and cleanest forms of energy generation. The use of fossil fuels such as coal, petroleum and natural gas has cost far more lives and created much more pollution than all the nuclear power stations in the world. This is not to say that nuclear energy is not potentially dangerous in the wrong hands. What this book aims to show is what happens when the rules surrounding nuclear power are ignored often with terrible results.

Whilst I believe renewable energy such as solar and wind can be a useful and important part of our power provision mix, anyone who thinks it can completely replace nuclear or fossil fuel power generation is badly mistaken. By 2035, this will become increasingly evident forcing the world to look again at nuclear energy as a prime power provider.

Disposal of the waste material from nuclear power stations is an ongoing problem. This is because much of it remains highly radioactive for thousands of years. Some of this waste can be recycled and reused as fuel. However, the bulk of it has to be buried in storage facilities such as the Waste Isolation Pilot Plant in New Mexico (*See Chapter 17*). This also does not address the problem that the quantity of radioactive waste grows by the year.

I believe that if nuclear energy continues to be a major power source, we will be forced to dispose of its waste by shooting it into outer space. This will be done by sending rockets loaded with nuclear waste to be exploded at the far edge of the solar system. Hardly an ideal solution, but is there an alternative? The answer is yes.

The other cleaner long term solution is to change the type of nuclear power we use to generate energy. Nuclear fusion is a safe, clean alternative to nuclear fission that is today's nuclear energy source. Whilst fusion does create a small amount of radioactive waste this has a much shorter life span than the waste from nuclear fission with its half-life of thousands of years. Like nuclear fission, nuclear fusion does not release any carbon emissions. It is also much safer than fission since it does not involve a chain reaction and cannot be used to manufacture nuclear weapons. The International Atomic Energy Agency estimates that a viable prototype fusion reactor will be built by 2040 and electricity generation by nuclear fusion will occur in the second half of the 21st Century.

Nuclear fusion occurs continuously in the solar system's greatest energy machine, namely the sun. It involves two hydrogen atoms known as deuterium and tritium combining to create helium which releases energy. In the sun, this occurs in an environment of extreme heat and pressure. To create fusion energy on earth, this environment has to be replicated somehow. This has yet to be achieved in a form that enables fusion to produce energy for commercial uses. Since the early 2000s, there are a number of companies working towards this extremely difficult and expensive goal. These include General Fusion, founded in Canada in 2009, which is developing a fusion power device based on magnetised target fusion to create totally clean energy.

In the U.K., First Light Fusion Ltd was spun out of scientific research departments at the University of Oxford in 2011 by Professor Yiannis Ventikos to create nuclear fusion energy. Its mission statement is: *Solving the problem of fusion power with the simplest machine possible.*

First Light Fusion is located near to Oxford and maintains a close relationship with the academic community. Their aim is to produce clean, affordable and virtually limitless fusion energy to power villages, towns and cities.

Tokamak Energy is another company that grew out of the scientific community, this time at Culham Laboratory in Oxfordshire, home of the world renowned JET energy research project. Their mission is also to achieve commercially viable fusion energy for commercial purposes. All these companies are racing to the magic goal of nuclear fusion reactors producing clean energy at an affordable cost to the consumer.

Assuming this goal is achieved I believe a likely future scenario will look like this:

By 2050 or 2060 renewable energy sources such as solar, wind and wave power will prove totally inadequate to provide the bulk of the earth's energy needs. This will force the world's nations to look again at nuclear energy as our prime power source. The nuclear fusion stations of this future will not be anything like today's giant plants. Instead, they will be discreet structures blending into the landscapes of the areas to which they supply power.

Using fusion rather than fission, production of much smaller quantities of short lived radioactive waste will make disposal considerably more manageable. If this comes to pass, the target of totally green energy will finally have been achieved. Moreover, nuclear disasters such as those that occurred at Mayak in the Urals and Three Mile Island will be things of the past.

An artist's impression of a fusion energy station
Image courtesy of First Light Fusion Ltd

Koeberg nuclear power station near Cape Town, South Africa.
Photograph by Nick Brazil

INDEX
People and Places

A-B

C - D

E - F

G - H

I - J

K-L

M - N

O - P

U - V

W - X

Y - Z

INDEX

Aircraft, Organisations,Vessels, All Other Items

A-C

D-G

H - J

K - M

N - P

Q - S

T - V

W - Z

Illustrations & Maps

Illustrations & Maps 2

Bibliography & Filmography

Full Body Burden: Growing Up in the Nuclear Shadow of Rocky Flats by Kristen Iversen is part memoir and part journalistic investigation into the history of The Rocky Flats Plant including the two big fires and the radiation leak at Pad 903. It is available from Amazon in Kindle, paperback and hardback editions.

"Lost Nuke - The Last Flight of Bomber 075" By Dirk Septer Heritage House Publishers ISBN Number 978-1-926936-87-1

Atomic Accidents: A History of Nuclear Meltdowns and Disasters: From the Ozarks to Fukushima by James Mahaffy
Pegasus Books

Voyage of The Lucky Dragon by Ralph E. Lapp Penguin Books 1957

A Review of Criticality Accidents 2000 LA-13638 Los Alamos National Laboratory

Secrets of The Conqueror Untold Secrets of Britain's Most Famous Submarine by Stuart Prebble Published by Faber & Faber 2012

Hiroshima by John Hersey First Published by New Yorker Magazine in 1946 Subsequently published by First Vintage Books in 1989. ISBN no: 0-679-72103-7

Nuclear Disaster In The Urals By Zhores Medvedev Published by W W Norton & Co 1980

Documentaries

City 40 - Documentary directed by Samira Goetschal about Ozersk & Mayak 2016 (Available on Netflix)

Mayak Half Life - Greenpeace documentary about Mayak and Muslumovo village 2002 (Available on You Tube)

Buzz One Four - Written, directed and narrated by Matt McCormick Available on Amazon Prime Video

Appendix

1) **Windscale Fire 1957 Radiation Release and Health Issues**
Subsequent research and investigations have revealed that the radiation released as a result of the Windscale Fire may have been greater than originally thought.
Three main radioactive isotopes were released as a result of the Wndscale Fire. They were as follows:
Iodine -131 - 740 Terabecquerels (Tbq) with a half life of 8 x days
Caesium -137 - 22 Tbq with a half life of 30 x years
Xenon - 133 - 12000 Tbq with a half life of 5.25 days
Small amounts of highly radioactive isotopes - plutonium and polonium 210 were also released.

The cloud of radioactive isotopes spread eastwards across North East England, Belgium, Norway and North Eastern Europe. The numbers of how many fatalities both long and short term were caused by the fire and radiation release vary. In 2007 on the 50th anniversary of the accident, a research paper by Richard Wakeford, visiting Professor at the University of Manchester's Dalton Nuclear Institute, and John Garland, formerly a researcher at the UK Atomic EnergynAuthority was released. On the basis of reassessing all the figures concerning the radiation leak, their paper concluded the amount of radiation released was twice the amount that was originally thought. On the basis of these revised figures they calculated that the numbers of fatalities could be between 100 and 240.

2) Greenham Common Air Crash 28th February 1958
Extract from Hansard, House of Commons
USAF Aircraft Accident, Greenham Common
5th March 1958
26.
Mr. Hurd
asked the Secretary of State for Air whether he will make a statement on the accident on 28th February at the Royal Air Force Station, Greenham Common, Newbury, in which B.47 bomber aircraft were involved.
Mr. Ward
I understand that a U.S.A.F. B.47 bomber developed engine trouble after

taking off from Greenham Common at about 4.30 last Friday afternoon. The pilot was obliged to jettison the wing tip fuel tanks, which fell into an emergency "dropping zone" where they would not normally have caused any harm. In this case, however, they unfortunately bounced into another B.47 aircraft on the ground and against a hangar and burst into flames. Two American airmen have since died from burns; eight others are injured. The bomber on the ground was destroyed, and the hangar severely damaged.The U.S.A.F. authorities have asked me to express their appreciation of the prompt assistance given by the local fire brigades who, with the R.A.F. and U.S.A.F. station fire services, brought the fire under control in about an hour.The U.S.A.F. take every practicable precaution to avoid risk from incidents of this kind and the fire at no time presented any danger to the local population. Civilian interests will be give full consideration during the Service Inquiry.

It is quite clear from this exchange resulting from a parliamentary question by Anthony Hurd, M.P. for Newbury at the time, that there was no government ‘cover up’ of the accident as has been alleged by various sources including Wikipedia. It should also be noted that this parliamentary answer by Mr Ward gives a full and accurate account of the accident less than a week after it happened. Whilst it does not mention whether or not the B-47 destroyed in the fire was carrying a nuclear weapon this could simply be for security reasons.

www.ingramcontent.com/pod-product-compliance
Ingram Content Group UK Ltd.
Pitfield, Milton Keynes, MK11 3LW, UK
UKHW020143250726
13967UKWH00002B/841